Prophets of Progress

Saint Simon, Comte & Spencer

Pioneers of Sociology

ISBN 1-903-499-84-4
978-1-903499-84-9

Printed and bound in the United Kingdom by
4edge Ltd, 7a Eldon Way Industrial Estate, Hockley, Essex, SS5 4AD.

Contents

Acknowledgment

This book is an updated, upgraded and refocused work based on an original MPhil thesis. Conducted on a part-time basis, the research was a daunting prospect. For that work, the author owes a special debt of gratitude to his director of studies, Mr Alan Watson, firstly for providing the opportunity to undertake the research, and secondly for his patient guidance and quietly exacting approach.

The focus of the original thesis was more explicitly on the scientific aspect of the theories. Whilst this still provides a powerful input, the current work has more to say on the utopian dimensions of the theories considered. This is reflected in a change of title from the rather dry sounding 'Spencer's Positivism and Evolutionism in Context' to the current 'Prophets of Progress, Saint Simon, Comte and Spencer'. Spencer still remains the key theorist to which the others provide the context of an alternative theoretical tradition within a different social context – and to a lesser extent vice versa.

Abstract

This text based research is a contribution to sociology which is concerned with the location of social theory within social and historical context rather than the question of its verification or falsification by some absolute criteria. The emphasis taken is that social theory relates to a social, cultural and intellectual tradition, is a product of a particular orientation of the theorist to certain social conditions, and that its fate is tied up with changes in these conditions. To appreciate the original relevance of theories which have become neglected due to social changes, it is therefore necessary to return to the originating social context and tradition within which they originated.

Herbert Spencer's theory of evolution and view of social progress is taken as a case study of this approach. His theory of change was used to analyse the past and the present and outline his utopian future. This research sketches the broad social and historical tradition as well as the more immediate context of Spencer's works, both of which provided a strong formative influence to Spencer's theoretical interpretation of social change.

The approach taken here emphasises that disagreements between the models of different theorists can be best understood as reflecting particular traditions. To illustrate this by providing a comparative backdrop, a brief contextual study is conducted of two theorists who shared with Spencer the desire to reduce the understanding of social history to that of social laws, but who constituted an opposing tradition. These theorists, Henri Saint Simon and Auguste Comte, were part of a peculiarly French tradition which culminated in the social theory of Emile Durkheim. The author makes no attempt to judge the contrasts, criticisms, misunderstandings and misrepresentations that abound between the French theorists and Spencer by the criteria of verification or falsification. Instead, it is made apparent that ethnocentrism was built into these theories, each of which claimed universal validity. Further, misunderstandings and misrepresentations are illustrated in a consideration of Durkheim's apparent refutation of Spencer. This indicates the importance of returning to Spencer's own works and of providing a contextual understanding of them.

Introduction

Aims of the text

This text looks at the way that pioneering social theory has developed within social and historical context with reference to a small number of theorists. The key figure of study is Herbert Spencer whose theory of social change will be located within mid nineteenth century England and the influences of his family and social class background. To help sharpen this analysis, a similar contextual approach will be taken, if in less detail, to the social theories developed by Henri Saint Simon and Auguste Comte within their French context.

Each of the theorists claimed to have developed a scientific understanding of the direction of social change from which could be anticipated a future ideal social condition. However, the theories of social change and the types of society that Spencer and the French writers argued were immanent were radically different, indicating their vast overgeneralizations from ethnocentric readings of history.

Opposing 'presentism' in social theory

According to the liberal social theorist and philosopher of science Karl Popper (1972), the hallmark of the physical sciences is that theories are formulated in such a way that they are open to rigorous testing and the possibility of falsification. Science evolves when, confronted with anomalous facts, a theory which is disproved becomes replaced by another with superior explanatory capacity which can account for both the terrain of facts of the old theory and those by which it was falsified. Any theory that is not open to the possibility of disproof by facts cannot be regarded as a science.

For Popper, a social science worthy of its name should evolve in similar fashion. If sociology progressed in this way, old theories, or parts of them, would only remain of value to the extent to which they had survived attempted falsification and been incorporated into contemporary theories with superior explanatory power. This would suggest a 'presentist' view of social theory; one which focusses on contemporary theory as surpassing past theories. The latter would be regarded as redundant and there would seem to be of little interest in explaining older theories within their historical context. Going back and studying these theories would be of little worth compared to an understanding of superior contemporary alternatives.

There has been much debate over whether the physical sciences advance in the way that Popper suggests (for example, Kuhn, 1962, and Feyerabend, 1975). Whether social science evolves in this way is highly debatable. For example, Szacki (1980), rejects the Popperian model of evolution in the social sciences, claiming that the progress of social knowledge is governed by different regularities to those of the natural sciences. In opposing the presentist view of sociology, he suggests a number of reasons for returning to a study of the classical sociological theorists. In particular, it is argued that the validity of social theory must be judged in terms of the social and historical circumstances of its formation.

In this text, it is argued that social theory does not advance in the manner that Popper proposes that the physical sciences do. The question of falsity in the social sciences is not necessarily clear cut or a matter of finality. Instead, its credibility relates to the social and historical conditions from which it originates and which provide the context for its evaluation. Changing social circumstances may seem to offer 'disproof' of a theory, but future social changes can come to suggest its growing relevance and provide some basis for its renaissance. Added to the questioning of the finality of truth or falsity in the social sciences, reasons for the retention or neglect of a social theory other than the simple test of falsification will be suggested. The author opposes the presentist view of social theory as both 1) implicated in an unrealistic view of its evolution and as 2) damaging to the acknowledgement of the sociological heritage.

The main interest here is not even essentially in trying to evaluate social theory in terms of its scientific truth. Rather, it is in rendering it comprehensible as the product of the desires of its creators within their micro and macro social and historical context. As a case study of this approach, interest is focussed upon the social theory of Herbert Spencer.

Spencer's social theory took its form from around the middle decades of the nineteenth century. Encapsulating the influences of Spencer's family background, it systematised a middle class, dissenting and entrepreneurial view of modernisation. Whether he proceeded scientifically is not the key question here, but within the context of a society engrossed in the achievements of science Spencer found it crucial to provide his resultant theory of social change with the kudos of scientific credibility. Through positing the existence of natural laws of evolution and social progress, Spencer utilised the notion of science to justify a contemporary form of free enterprise capitalism and provide optimism in its radicalisation and future extension toward a perfectly rounded social form. The fortune of Spencer's social theory was thus bound up with its predictive nature and the success of the social forces that he sided with and hoped to advance. As it turned out, an alternative direction of social change would explain its demise around the turn of the twentieth century and neglect between the 1930s and 1960s. However, it gained revived academic attention during the period of new right Conservative government in Britain in the 1980s and 1990s.

One problem of the presentist view of social theory is that by claiming that a theory has been superseded it discourages studying the theory in its original form. Any misrepresentations of it are thus more likely to be accepted and perpetuated. Such, it has been argued (Jones, 1974), has been the fate of Spencer since his ideas were eclipsed in the late nineteenth century by the criticisms of Emile Durkheim.

Durkheim's theory, like Spencer's, was a product of its historical and social environment. In this case, it was in a tradition of scientific sociology attuned to both explain and attempt to influence French modernisation. Choosing between these theories is thus less a matter of some criteria of overall scientific truth than of pacing them within different social and intellectual traditions that they reflected and articulated. Furthermore, it could be argued that if Durkheim's theory surpassed Spencer's, it was mainly because he lived to have, at the time, the last word.

In terms of its interest within the academic world, a social theory may fall into neglect for a number of other reasons. One is that it may not fit neatly into a theory of the development of sociology. It will be shown that Spencer's theory provided this problem for both Nisbet (1970b) and Gouldner (1977) and was consequently virtually screened out of their analyses.

Historicism

Another problem for Spencer's social theory has been what might be interpreted as an embarrassed silence by liberal social theorists who have been strong to condemn 'historicism'. Popper (1974, p.3) has defined historicism as 'an approach to the social sciences which assumes that *historical prediction* is their principal aim, and which assumes that this aim is attainable by discovering the 'rhythms' or the 'patterns', the 'laws' or the 'trends' that underlie the evolution of history'.

Popper associated historicism with an illegitimate holistic approach to the study of society and the reading of social history on a grand scale from which it was claimed could be extracted laws of change which pointed to utopian futures. Hayek, (1952) a fellow liberal, identified 'scientism' - an inappropriate and hubristic application of science to the social world – with social holism and a desire for control that has close affinities with totalitarianism. For these theorists, the holism associated with historicism made its claims to the discovery of social laws to be founded on unscientific procedures because rather than based on facts laws could only be grasped intuitively. However, the problem that Spencer's social theory posed for these theorists was that it was scientistic, historicist and utopianist, but it was also radically liberal.

This work in relation to others

Some writers present founding theorists in the light of contemporary (at the time!) sociological thought which it is believed will have sifted out dated and 'irrelevant' aspects of their work from contributions which remain of continuing relevance. Rumney (1966), in the Forward to his classic exposition of Spencer, explicitly adopted this approach. Another version of this stance was advocated by Andreski (1972, p.7) who believed that insights of founding theorists could be selectively appropriated by the test of time and fitted together to form an accurate picture of the social world. Such a 'survival of the fittest' approach to ideas is not the purpose of this work. It implies that either the selected features of the theory are of enduring value or that the future progress of knowledge will continue to reduce the truth content of the theory. Both options, it is argued, are untenable representations of the ebbs and flows of social theory which accompany social change.

Many works aim to popularise a founding theorist by emphasising the enduring significance of and our indebtedness to their works. One approach has been to select and edit sections of the theorist's work believed to exhibit greatest clarity and power of exposition. The selections are usually preceded by the editor's defence of the theorist. A classic example of this is Fletcher's (1974) presentation of Comte's early works. Others include Thompson (1976) (on Comte), Ionescu (1976) and Markham (1952) (on Saint Simon), and Andreski (1972) and Carneiro (1967) (on Spencer). From the perspective of this writer, such partisanship risks neglecting an appraisal of the validity of the works relative to their originating historical context.

The author's position is closer to that adopted by Peel whose major work on Spencer (1971) does not focus on differentiating 'true' though from 'corrupt' as the test of a theory's durability (Preface, xi – xii). Peel's aim is to aid our understanding of social theory by portraying the theorist in the context of an age that may be alien to us. To this, it could be added that an age does not necessarily become increasingly alien in linear fashion with the extension of time. Once neglected theories may thus regain attention as once again more relevant, almost as if being rediscovered.

Historical context approaches of a broader range include those of Coser, Gouldner and Nisbet. Coser's (1977) sociological study of founding sociologists locates theorists and their central ideas in their micro and macro social context. But within these contexts, Coser tends to compartmentalise the theorists and their ideas; he does not as his main aim use one theorist for the purposes of bringing out the ideas of another.

Gouldner (1977) relates the emergence of sociology to the need to form coherent social maps during times of change and uncertainty. He argues that whilst social theory may appear to be a conscious logical construction which should be evaluated by the canons of scientific method, there is always a less conscious sub-theoretical (metaphysical) level of background assumptions which may give the theory appeal and affect its success irrespective of its logical validity. The author has some sympathy with this position, but not Gouldner's dismissal of Spencer because he was supposedly not a 'characteristic thinker' (1977, p.117) of the classical period of sociology.

For Nisbet, the pioneers of 'The Sociological Tradition' (1970b) rooted its general perspective in a response to tendencies of social dispersal unleashed by the French and Industrial Revolutions. He argues that preoccupation with the question of a new social order led to the rediscovery of medievalism and established sociology on a basis of conservative concepts. This interpretation makes sense within the French context and the works of Saint Simon and Comte, but again leads to the virtual dismissal of Spencer as a significant figure because he does not fit the developmental model. From the vantage point that is adopted by the author in this text, Nisbet seems to make an over simplistic equation between the social phenomena of the two revolutions and the sociological responses to them.

Central concepts

Positivism

Each of the main theorists considered in this work have been referred to as 'positivists'. The meaning of the term 'positivism', as used in sociology, must therefore be explored. It essentially refers to the epistemological position that society can be studied in a similar scientific fashion to the phenomena of the natural sciences. However, one problem, highlighted by Giddens (1974, Preface) is that it has become a highly pejorative and ambiguous term since its inception in the works of Comte. For example, positivists became the target of attack from supporters of more subjectivist approaches to sociology such as symbolic interactionism, ethnomethodology and phenomenology that were making their mark during the 1960s and 1970s. For ethnomethodologists in particular, the term positivism was often used as a term of abuse, hurled at those sociologists whose approach was to apply statistical analysis to the study of what was misleadingly claimed to be factual social data.

In fact, the latter approach may more appropriately referred to as empiricism. As will be shown, Comte expressly argued against the simple application of mathematics to the analysis of social phenomena (Martineau, 1855, p.492). Nevertheless, remarkable misrepresentations have since been made of Comte's position. For example, Bogardus (1940, p.243) asserted that for Comte 'mathematics is the best tool for obtaining social accuracy' and Pollard (1971, pp.119-120) emphasised Comte's reliance on statistics and probability as the basis for establishing social laws.

As well as referring to an approach to science appropriate to the study of society, the term positivism has been used by Comte to herald a future social order, a positivist era, and also associated with his religion of humanity and the positivist church. In its nineteenth century context, Halfpenny (1982, Ch.1) has distinguished six usages of the term and Charlton (1959, pp.12-11) four. To this can be added that during the twentieth century, the varied use of the term positivism in sociology and philosophy has also led to much confusion.

The close association of positivism with the works of Comte led his theoretical opponent Spencer to disavow its application to his own works (Spencer, 1968). However, it is quite possible to base a definition of the term on points of commonality which existed between these theorists. In each there resided the belief that social phenomena operated in a law like way and are amenable to 'scientific' understanding. They argued that the procedures of the natural sciences could be adapted to the study of social phenomena with theoretical explanations and social predictions grounded in the phenomena. Any social theories which could not be thus grounded were viewed as straying into the realm of metaphysics or religion.

Giddens (1977, p.30) has provided a concise definition of positivism. As he puts it, central to nineteenth century positivism resided the 'conviction that all 'knowledge', or all that was to count as 'knowledge' is capable of being expressed in terms which refer in an immediate way to some reality, or aspects of reality that can be apprehended through the senses' and a 'faith that the methods and logical structure of science, as epitomized in classical physics, can be applied to the study of social phenomena'. This usually implies social theories of the macro level that explain social phenomena in terms of impersonal mechanical laws and which disregards the subjective viewpoint of individual members of society.

The author's one reservation to Giddens' definition is that in the second quotation the term 'applied' risks caricaturing these theorists and the term 'adapted' is preferred. Our theorists were each aware of particular problems for the scientific study of social phenomena. Further, we should beware of viewing these theorists as rigid scientistic analysts of the macro order only. In the following quotation, a strongly interpretive viewpoint is adopted:

'There is no more mischievous absurdity than this judging of actions from the outside as they look to us, instead of from the inside as they look to the actors; nothing more irrational than to criticise deeds as though the doers of them had the same desires, hopes, fears, and restraints with ourselves. We cannot understand another's character except by abandoning our own identity, and realizing to ourselves his frame of mind' (Spencer, 1970, pp.228-229).

As indicated, the sociologist was in fact Herbert Spencer! Much of his later written Principles of Sociology he considered an attempt to apply such an approach to understanding the life and outlook of man in 'primitive' times. He equated this approach with scientific open mindedness – but proceeded in an arguably unscientific way to subordinate his interpretations of primitive psychology to the verification of his impersonal laws of evolution!

Progress

Progress refers to change that is evaluated as betterment (Ginsberg, 1973, Ch.1). Betterment may be defined and measured by such criteria as knowledge, civilisation, quality of life and material comfort. However, there is some disagreement over the historical origin of the notion of progress. For Nisbet (1970a, Introduction) and Bock (in Bottomore & Nisbet (ed), 1978), images of progress and evolution have long been associated with the metaphor of growth and decay and the view that all change takes place in natural life cycles. This cyclical outlook, which included a view of social change, was recognized by the ancient Greeks and was sometimes applied even to the extent of anticipating a literal repetition of events that had taken place in history. For Nisbet and Bock, the recognition of progress was apparently evident to the ancients in the upward phase of the cycle. However, Pollard (1971, p.16) has maintained that since the cyclical view suggested endless repetitions, the idea of progress as relentless advance could not have been generalized from it. Bury concurred, stating that, regarding progress, 'this idea means that civilization has moved, is moving, and will move in a desirable direction' (1920, p.2) indefinitely. Consequently, he argued that the idea of progress can only have emerged with the breaking down of the cyclical view of change.

Christian theologians of the Middle Ages often retained a cyclical view in which the future was seen as the degeneration phase of a massive cycle (Nisbet, 1970a, Ch.2). From this viewpoint, despite, or even because of material advance, man was degenerating from past spiritual purity toward future apocalypse. Notions of utopia thus far related either to the past, to heaven, or to some distant dream island.

What is clear is that by the late seventeenth century, rationalist thinkers were becoming impressed by the prospect of an endless advance in scientific knowledge. In this regard, Fontenelle's key work of 1688 ('A Digression on the Ancients and Moderns') is widely regarded as a crucial contribution toward breaking the cyclical view of change (Bury, 1920, Ch.5). The cyclical outlook, and that of the 'ancients', who looking back in time considered the achievements of classical civilizations as unsurpassable, became increasingly undermined by the powerful idea of ongoing upward social change with the decay of old age never arising. If human genius was constant, cultural advance was cumulative, with each generation building on the inheritance of the cultural knowledge and achievements of its predecessors; a process destined to continue indefinitely into the future. This optimistic view of the 'moderns' became in time broadened out and related to technological and material progress, moral progress, and progress in a rational and scientific understanding of society itself. Via especially the French Enlightenment philosophers and also Scottish Enlightenment writers, it culminated in the works of those nineteenth century positivists who viewed history as revealing a law like direction of progress, carrying society forward toward a future secular utopia. When positivism and the notion of progress were combined, positivism provided progress with the substance of objective science, and progress contributed the value judgement of betterment. Together, they claimed to offer a compass bearing for practical social policy guidance, above short term political manoeuvrings, to assist the steering of society, easing its course toward its scientifically established future destination.

It took the pessimistic climate of the early decades of the twentieth century for anti-positivist cyclical theories to re-emerge in the writings of Spengler and Toynbee (Sorokin, 1963, Chs.4-5). For these Christian writers, civilisation dominated by science and technology represented an icy condition of moral decay at the bottom end of a historical cycle. Indeed, their very understanding of history emphasised the importance of its intuitive grasp as opposed to scientific understanding. They looked forward to the upsurge of a new religious beginning of creative and charismatic leadership.

More recently, theorists loosely bracketed as postmodernists have attacked positivism from the viewpoint that the Enlightenment promise of progressive human liberation was unfulfilled in societies of the modern era. From this viewpoint, as we enter the postmodern age, it is apparent that there are no laws of social change that enable the future social condition to be predicted – there have only been attempts by powerful groups to claim the superiority of science to impose their model of reality on others.

Evolution

Evolution has been defined as growth which is internally engendered (Ginsberg, 1973, Ch.5; Nisbet, 1970a, Ch.4). The motive force for evolutionary change is the inbuilt tendency for the unfolding of a potential which has resided in the nature of the phenomena from its inception. When applied to social change, this apparently natural process, whilst postulated abstractly, may be difficult to construct from the study of concrete societies, each of which display real world impediments. It therefore arguably requires insightful understanding of processes involved on a grand scale.

Social evolutionists have identified a variety of essences as the motor of change which usually imply evolution through conflict or struggle resulting in the realization of a social type in which the fulfilment of the potential in human nature can fully unfold. For Marx, for example, compared to the experience of alienation under capitalism, class conflict would drive social change toward communism, a form of society which would enable the full realisation of man's 'species being'.

By contrast, the height of evolution for Spencer was his model industrial society of small enterprise capitalism. A condition of enlightened individualism – enabling the freedom of self-supporting individuals, each not transgressing the like freedoms of other similarly enlightened individuals – was man's moral potential which Spencer argued could only be realized in the fully evolved industrial society. It would be brought about through the changing nature of the 'survival of the fittest' from that of militant conflict between organised collectives to one of peaceful competition between industrious individuals.

Nineteenth century social evolutionists have commonly been regarded as adopting a 'unilinear' approach to social change, positing the existence of laws of change in natural history (Nisbet, 1970a, Ch.4 & p.165). From this viewpoint, there is a single natural line of social change and predicted future social destiny. Along this line could be arranged societies as more or less advanced. This unilinear emphasis would suggest that the differences between contemporary societies were a result of different stages of growth reached along a common fixed path in relation to specific obstacles encountered (Nisbet, 1970a, Ch.5).

Such a view of evolution as a process of change along a singular scale has tended to come into disrepute. However, even unilinearism did not necessarily mean that all societies had to pass through the same rigid sequential stages of evolution. This tends to be a mistaken criticism of the unilinearism of nineteenth century social philosophers who applied their laws on a grand scale to the natural history of societies in ensemble, taken from the vantage point of twentieth century sociologists who took society itself as their unit of analysis.

Furthermore, applied to the works of Spencer, the charge of unilineraism has been challenged by Haines (1988) who argues that Spencer's works combine an awareness of immanent change with that of environmental contingency. Similarly, Sahlins and Service (1973, Foreward, Ch.1 & 2) have attempted to rehabilitate evolutionism by bringing out the theme of 'multilinear' or 'specific' evolution detectable in the works of nineteenth century theorists, but which often remained unrecognized through their conceptualisation as unilinearists. Multilinearism focussed on explaining social diversity in terms of evolutionary adaptation of societies to their specific environmental influences (specific evolution) such as geography, climate, isolation, relations with other societies etc. Rather than viewed simply in terms of advance along a universal and unilinear scale of natural evolution (general evolution), particular societies could be seen as branching in different directions and studied in terms of adaptation to their specific environment in their actual historical setting. For Sahlins and Service, both processes are operative in the form of 'grand evolution'.

Technically, 'evolution itself......does not necessarily mean, applied to society, the movement of man to a desirable goal. It is a neutral, scientific conception, compatible either with optimism or pessimism' (Bury, 1920, p.335). But evolution and the more evaluative idea of progress, whilst conceptually distinguishable, are certainly not mutually exclusive for our theorists. Indeed, they tend to be mutually inclusive. Thus, whilst for Comte social progress was related to the advance of science applied to the social realm, the essence of social change resided in the capacity of the mind to advance to new stages of thinking through its intolerance of irreconcilable modes of thinking regarding different levels of phenomena. And whilst Spencer was the evolutionist supreme, he was also a utopianist with a clear view of social and moral progress. He made sure of intertwining evolution and progress.

According to Nisbet (1970a), however, the main appeal of evolutionism was its unilinearism. Nineteenth century positivism combined with the notion of progress and evolution emphasised inevitability, universality and scientific grounding of social knowledge in laws of change. Theories combining these characteristics projected a model social future as a universal outcome. To the intellectual appeal of social scientific theory and prediction was harnessed the emotional appeal of reassurance that history was on the side of particular social forces and the attraction of a future utopia. For Saint Simon and Comte, that future held a withdrawal from individualism; for Spencer, an extension of individualism. Behind these contrasting utopias resided the theorists' different views on the nature, progress and role of social science, the pace of social change and its driving force, the realisation of an ideal moral condition and the basis for perfect social stability.

Utopianism

Utopia is arguably the most value laden of the concepts introduced in this section. It embraces a dreamlike and powerful image quality of existence under conditions of perfect fulfilment and, shaped by the times and cultural environment of writers, has taken various forms throughout history. For example, Kumar points out that Plato's image of utopia was a hierarchical society governed by a philosophical elite. By contrast, More's was a democratic community in which all would experience the good life through common and moderate engagement in labour to benefit both body and mind. In such a society, the quest was for peace, a simple life and spirituality (Kumar, 1991, pp.48–50).

During medieval times, society was experienced as relatively static and divinely ordered. Images of utopia left little scope for the idea of a perfect future condition or an existence designed and implemented by man. Utopian images may have referred to mythical past conditions or imagined existing far off lands. They often held religious connotations, envisaging environments which enhanced spiritual development. If the future was envisaged, it would likely be portrayed as the product of divine intervention.

It was from the time of the European Enlightenment, especially the French strand, that the view strongly emerged that utopia was within future grasp through rational design. The advance of scientific reasoning, technology and industry would come to be allied with utopian images of future societies. Science would both 'prove' the direction of progress toward utopia through establishing laws of historical change and provide the basis for a society of social harmony and the means of plenty. Utopias had now become 'directional fantasy-images of possible futures'

(Elias, 1981, quoted in Kilminster, p.6, Available at: http://quod.lib.umich.edu/h/humfig/11217607.0003.2*?rgn=full+text Accessed 12 February 2015). But what was the direction of social change and what was the natural outcome of the unfolding of the laws of change in the high point society of the future? Here, the appeal of science, within different social and historical conditions, could be used to point to and thus justify quite different social outcomes and provide inspirations for people to act in such a way as to enhance these outcomes. Allied with utopia, science acquired a powerful ideological component and itself provided an element of certainty.

Kumar (1987, p.52), puts this point succinctly. With reference to nineteenth century theorists of social progress, he states that:

'In the very language they use, in the whole style and manner of presentation, it is obvious that they are in the business not just of scientific explanation but of exhortation. For whatever reasons of personal, class or national circumstances, they are concerned to urge upon us a particular interpretation of the industrializing process, to put upon it a peculiar colour, bias, and pressure'.

Regarding the supposed scientific basis claimed for their theories of change, he goes on to say that 'Often, too, the source of that interpretation seems to lie as much in artistic intuition, and in particular glimpses and insights, as in the scientific accumulation and examination of evidence' (Kumar, 1987, p.52). And the selective view of the theorists is emphasised when Kumar (1987, p.53) goes on to refer to them as 'thinkers who have had a particular vision of the newly-emerging order, a vision which has vividly lit up particular features of the landscape while relegating others to the shadows'.

Touching on what is to come
In this work, at the macro level, the writer will be locating Spencer's social theory within its social and historical context. The aim will be to clarify the specifically English context of the theory. This can be brought out by viewing it as a critical response to the different pattern of French modernisation reflected in the positivism of Henri Saint Simon and Auguste Comte. In terms of the evaluative criteria of progress and evolution built into Spencer's theory, French traditions of Catholicism, state interventionism, collectivism, and the experience of revolution and reaction compared unfavourably with the English Protestant tradition, constitutional freedoms, industrialisation in the form of free enterprise and possessive individualism, and gradual modernisation – and of

course the reverse was applicable, especially from the viewpoint of Comte.

Cultural and intellectual traditions both reflect and influence social conditions. They also form important resources from which theorists draw. The French Enlightenment, in the works of the philosophes, came to provide an attack in the form of rational criticism on Catholic dogma and obscurantism. Their ideas were a contributory factor to the Revolution of 1789. Saint Simon's and Comte's positivism can be regarded as a theoretical partial reaction to the ideas of the philosophes and the Revolution. In the search for a theoretical basis for a new post-Revolution social order, their theories combined an explanation of revolutionary change within a framework of rationality and progress, but also with a reverence for tradition.

Like their French counterparts, writers in the tradition of the Scottish Enlightenment, for example Miller and Ferguson, developed ideas of natural historical progress. However, in succeeding the 'revolutions' of the seventeenth century, which had already brought about a relatively modern constitution to England, a degree of religious tolerance and advances in free enterprise commerce, the tone of these writers was more one of optimism in evolutionary progress through the civilising influence of a commercial society. It was the mechanics of the emerging free enterprise society that political economists such as Adam Smith focussed on. As a pointer to further social progress, Spencer broadened out Smith's economic model into a social model which in radicalised form provided for him an image of an ideal future. Basing his theory of evolution on a particular view of English modernisation, Spencer did not have to make the extremes of revolution and tradition central to his explanation of change. In contrast to Comte's theory, Spencer's theory of natural social change combined gradualism with a powerful strand of anti-traditionalism. From Spencer's viewpoint, Comte's positivism held a view of the future which was too contaminated with (a particular model of) the past.

For Saint Simon, and especially Comte, the condition of society and its course of change were ultimately governed by the state of intellectual thinking and world views which hold sway over people's lives and shape their outlooks. Such a theoretical reading of the social condition is referred to in sociology as an 'idealist' approach. Both writers acutely felt that they were living in a period of post-Revolution social and moral crisis. They diagnosed this crisis to have originated in the collapse of the intellectual cohesion that supported the old order through the philosophe's attack on the world view of Catholicism. For them, this attack precipitated the Revolution. To curtail the consequent social and moral crisis, a new socially integrating cohesive intellectual outlook had to be established.

By contrast, for Spencer, man's moral condition was a modifiable and inbuilt quality. It is this internal moral quality which ultimately determines the acceptability of social ideas and the necessary level of social constraints that would be required for social order to subsist. By the criteria of Spencer's theory, both the French Revolution and the subsequent need and desire for a new regulated social and altruistic moral order and social dogma were a measure of moral immaturity. In this post-Revolution context, French positivism amounted to the search for a new repressive dogma to replace the old one of Catholicism and to curb a moral condition of egoistic selfishness.

Compared to the French experience, in England a condition of relative social cohesion had combined itself with the advance of individual freedom. In Spencer's scheme, this combination indicated a state of relative moral maturity which was associated with industrial success; individual enterprise and responsibility was bringing to Britain economic prosperity, and this outlook was confidently projected by Spencer in his first major work, Social Statics (1970), originally published in 1850 during the heyday of Victorian free enterprise and prosperity. For Spencer, the future confidently lay in the extension of the free market. The pioneers of this future were the provincial middle classes of Spencer's own background. An analysis of the latter will therefore be necessary to establish the values which animated Spencer's vision of a future utopia and shaped his social science.

To approach the task that the author has set for this text, a significant proportion of the work requires a prior appraisal of Saint Simon's and Comte's social theory with reference to its French social historical setting. A basis is thereby established for appraising the nature of Spencer's social theory in its peculiarly English context.

Spencer devoted a number of essays in whole or part to a criticism of Comte's positivism (see Ch.5) but there is no evidence that Spencer was familiar with Saint Simon's works other than by reputation. He never made more than a passing reference to the theorist (for example, 1975, Pt.8, Ch. 22). The author has nevertheless included a section on Saint Simon. He was part of the French interventionist tradition that Spencer clearly loathed. As Comte's mentor and arguably sharing a similar analysis of the French social and moral condition, Saint Simon can be linked closely with Comte as a pioneer of a French positivist tradition which runs through to Durkheim. In the conclusion to this work, Durkheim's criticism of Spencer is used to further clarify the latter's social theory.

Although embedded within a particular tradition, the fate of Spencer's social theory can also be related to changing social conditions in England. It was the product of both a time and a class outlook. In his early works, Spencer optimistically opposed the interventionist arm of the English Enlightenment in the form of utilitarianism. He later opposed the interventionism of New Liberal thinking and what he referred to as the 'Toryism' of Liberal governments, feared that the growing influence of the working class could lead to socialism, and opposed the revival of militarism around the turn of the twentieth century. This forms a changing social context to which continuities and changes in his social theory can be related.

In this work, sketches of French and English history are provided for contextual purpose. The author is fully aware that there is no such thing as a pure interpretation of history. Each of the theorists reviewed in this work had their own reading of history which both shaped and was shaped by the theories of progress and evolution that they developed. How accurate their theories were is not the primary aim of this work, but rather to both understand them and the social context of their formation. Therefore, if it appears that the views of history sketched in the English and French chapters are shaped as being seen through the eyes of the theorists, this is argued as beneficial to the aims of the work rather than problematic.

Prophets of Progress: Saint Simon, Comte and Spencer

1 | A Sketch of the French Historical Background to the Theory of Saint Simon and Comte

This chapter sets the social and historical scene for an appreciation of the influences which shaped the social theory of Henri Saint Simon and Auguste Comte. Although their theories of social progress claimed universal application, it will enable us to recognize specifically French aspects of their formation. Another historical sketch will later set the English context of Spencer's social theory. We will then be in a position to appraise Spencer's theory within both its English context and as a comment on the nature of French modernization and as a response to these French theorists. To gain credence for a particular view of social progress and the type of society which was to be its destination, each of these theorists adopted a positivistic epistemology, using the appeal to scientific certainty.

Compared to England, feudalism in France was relatively vibrant and enduring. From its height around the twelfth century, this system comprised a social hierarchy of closed strata in which the Catholic Church (the first estate) and the nobility (the second estate) constituted the privileged orders. Hereditary social power and privilege over the third order (artisans, traders and, in particular, peasants) followed the inheritance of land ownership and noble title. Power was essentially localized in the nobility (Tocqueville, 1966), with the monarch recognized as a superior amongst nobles.

The nobility and the church placed a heavy burden of taxation and labour requirements on a largely landless peasantry who were held in perpetual servitude. The nobility legitimized their position and privileges in the feudal social hierarchy through their role in administration, the dispensing of justice and the protection of the lower orders. Upholding their position in the social hierarchy was sustained by a backward looking view. Tracing their noble genealogies back over many generations was best 'proof' of their superior social breeding and, importantly, involvement in 'base' business activity risked derogation from noble station.

The Catholic clergy preached that the social order was divinely appointed. They thus complemented the nobility in supporting the hierarchy and traditions of feudalism and the higher offices recruited exclusively from those of wealthy background. In a country relatively immune from the critical influence of the Reformation, feudalism and Catholicism in France remained relatively deep rooted.

What did emerge out of feudalism and contribute to its undermining was a growing concentration of power in the form of royal absolutism, the extent of which clearly distinguished late feudalism in France from that in England (Anderson, 1984). For centuries, the balance of power between the French monarch and the nobility had oscillated. Whenever possible, the nobility asserted their local power and independence, but occasionally a determined monarch would impose central authority. Royal absolutism became extended further on each occasion of its assertion, reaching its height during the late seventeenth and early eighteenth centuries under Louis XIV (Anderson, 1984, Ch.4). It was supported by the religious sanction of divine right rule and in return monarchs firmly prescribed Catholicism as the national religion. Religious non-adherents often faced vicious persecution. Some, such as communities of Huguenots, settled in England. Early modernist writers, who saw in man's rational capacity the basis for social progress, faced severe censorship (Brumfitt, 1972, Ch.3).

The effective imposition of royal authority required the development of a centralized state apparatus. Through this apparatus, high government office and accompanying noble status (nobility of the chancery) and privileges were open to purchase. Decrees, administrative courts and taxation increasingly derived from the centre as government regulation reached down to involvement in local matters through the appointment of officials called intendants (Tocqueville, 1966, Pt.2, Chs.1,2,5,6,& 7). As a result, the nobility were losing their traditional local role, but clinging to their privileges. In this way, their legitimacy was being undermined at the same time that the peasantry were increasingly suffering under the weight of an extra level of taxation deriving from the centre (Tocqueville, 1966, Pt.2, Ch.1).

Anderson (1984) has characterised royal absolutism as a transitional phase on the road to capitalism. In the French case, it was accompanied by growing financial crisis. Attempting to address the problem through the neo-feudal strategy of the sale of office fuelled the growth of the administrative structure. This process arguably diverted talent away from business enterprise and locked it into a system of privilege offering hereditary security of the office owned irrespective of merit.

Following the death of Louis XIV in 1715, censorship became somewhat relaxed, and a number of French writers were openly expressing their admiration for English political liberties and commercial freedoms. From this time dates the influential writings of Voltaire and other figures of literary ability to whom government posts were not open on intellectual merit (Tocqueville, 1966, Pt.3, Ch.1). This 'alienated' intelligentsia, the 'philosophes', became most industrious in their output by the middle decades to the eighteenth century. They did not produce a common coherent doctrine, but in the Enlightenment tradition as social philosophers, they invariably admired the achievements of science and shared the moderns' optimism in human progress through the application of reason. In the hands of the philosophes, these ideas became a powerful weapon of attack against remaining irrational feudal traditions and the religious obscurantism of clerics.

Voltaire, who had visited England, may be regarded as a representative figure of emerging bourgeois values. He inveighed against both the entrenched pro-feudal outlook of sections of the nobility and the dogma and intolerance of Catholic clericism. For Voltaire, progress required the dismantling of the remnants of feudalism (Brumfitt, 1972, Ch.4), the putting of government finances in order, the guaranteeing of private property rights and the encouragement of commerce. However, disdainful of the uneducated masses, he opposed this stratum as a possible revolutionary force and did not advocate the extension of democracy. For Voltaire, the masses would continue to need some form of religion and absolutist governance to maintain social order and their control. Modernisation through the institution of enlightened royal absolutism seemed to be the key to the progress of the commercial classes and the control of the other orders.

Other facets of Enlightenment thinking included a cataloguing of the achievements of reason by Diderot and d'Alembert in the Encyclopaedia, the first volume of which appeared in 1751. The atheistic critics in particular challenged the church view, held by Catholic traditionalists, of the essential wickedness in man which had to be suppressed. This particular fixed view of human nature denied the possibility of human progress. Instead, critics proposed that the potential good in man could be enhanced through improvement of the social environment, guided by rational analysis. For many Enlightenment writers, such as the atheist Diderot, the ultimate aim in the realisation of the good in human nature was to rationally redesign society to maximise human happiness.

An emphasis on the optimistic view that the human condition can be improved through improving the social environment was a feature of Condillac's 'sensationalism', which posited that knowledge was not innate, as maintained by Catholic traditionalists, but derived from the senses. Helvetius, sharing the outlook of achieving the greatest happiness of the greatest number, emphasised the key role of education as the vehicle of human improvement.

Despite his early involvement in the Encyclopaedia project, Rousseau is usually regarded as standing apart from the other philosophes, not sharing their optimism in basing the progress of civilisation on rational thinking. For Rousseau, civilisation must be reconciled with man's feelings and emotions if it is to be beneficial.

Condorcet, writing later in the eighteenth century, was an atheist philosopher of progress who built on the ideas of Turgot, and argued that mathematics would be the foundation of social analysis in the immanent future. Ironically, during the reign of terror phase of the French Revolution, justified by reference to Rousseau's notion of the 'general will', Condorcet suffered imprisonment and death under Maximilien Robespierre. (Brumfitt, 1972, Chs.6 & 7 and Mornet, 1969, Pt.5, Ch.2 provide excellent references to the ideas of the Enlightenment philosophes).

Despite their usual pro-monarchism, works not upholding traditional religious dogma ran the risk of censorship and those involved in their production faced possible imprisonment or exile. However, because by the 1770s such suppressions became often only half-heartedly imposed, they were arguably counterproductive since, in a climate of growing boldness, the risk to publish was often taken and if censorship were imposed great fame was often brought to the works of the victims (Mornet, 1969, Pt.5, Ch.2).

Tocqueville (1966) has maintained that through their exclusion from high office, the ideas of the philosophes were pitched at the level of abstract criticisms, unrefined by the practicalities of political experience. As such, they tended to apply rational criticism to sweepingly condemn past traditions and offer impractical utopian visions of future social perfection, placing European societies at the forefront of humanity. Nevertheless for Mornet (1969, Pt.3), their advocacy of experimental science and observation have often been underplayed.

Supporters of bourgeois reform, including enlightened nobles, all commonly excluded from access to the practicalities of high government office, often found pleasure in discussing radical ideas in the abstract in the fertile meeting grounds of the salons, the abstract nature of the ideas offering an element of safety. The tidal wave of critical literature and discussion generated increasing optimism in the possibility of rationally directed progress, especially in the context of the self-indulgent and revenue squandering court life of Louis XV (Salvemini, 1963, pp. 47-56).

Louis XVI, who came to the throne in 1774, appeared to recognize the need for social reform to tackle the mounting revenue problem. The appointment of Turgot, a philosopher of progress and supporter of free market reforms, as Comptroller-General was a move to overhaul the tax system that won great praise from Voltaire (Brumfitt, 1972, p153). However, recognizing the threat to their traditional privileges and exemptions that reform would bring, the court nobility closed ranks and

Turgot fell from office largely through their machinations (Salvemini, 1963, pp.92-93; Williams, 1970, p.239). With the loss of a philosopher of progress from such high office, the pressures for reform from above had eased. The nobility subsequently attempted to close ranks to protect themselves from further threats to their privileges, but there is disagreement as how effective their actions were. Salvemini, (1963, pp.98-99) suggests that a significant defensive reaction was effected, whilst Barrington Moore (1967, pp.66-67) argues that the changes were more of legal formality than social substance. Those who follow Salvemini's position argue that the effective exclusion of the moneyed bourgeoisie from purchasing government office and the privileges and status of noble rank that accompanied it encouraged them to become further alienated from feudal privilege and attracted to the ideas of the philosophes – a precipitating factor in the Revolution that was to come.

From the late 1770s, the ideas of the philosophes were gaining fashion. They were discussed openly in enlightened society, with ideas overheard in conversation even percolating down to illiterate servants (Mornet, 1969, Pt.5, Chs.4, 5 & 6). Although few of the philosophes were desirous of outright revolution, much talk abounded of its prospects, likelihood and even inevitability.

Tocqueville (1966, Pt.3, Ch.4) has convincingly argued that, on the eve of the Revolution, the increased burden of taxation that had been placed on the peasantry stoked resentment against persisting feudal privileges and that their own privations had been heightened against a background of rising expectations that had accompanied a sustained growth in prosperity and the prospect of reform during the previous decades. Attempted administrative reforms from the centre had brought widespread chaos, uncertainty (Tocqueville, 1966, Pt.3, Ch.7) and furthermore encouraged obstructionism by vested noble interests. Sections of the pro-feudal nobility even hoped to use the crisis to their advantage to reinvigorate feudalism. The effects of the harvest failure of 1788 on the peasantry (Williams, 1970, p.225; Salvemini, 1963, pp.119-120) and the breakdown in administration only increased the hardship of the lower orders and resentment grew in the face of dashed expectations of reform.

The growth of centralized administration had meanwhile largely undermined the once perceived legitimacy of the local feudal order. With the collapse of the administrative centre, the ancien regime cataclysmically collapsed (Tocqueville, 1966, Pt.3, Ch.7). The reins of power at the National Assembly were taken up largely by jurists and bourgeois landowners, the latter with much to guard against losing as well as to gain from revolutionary change. But they and the rest of what had been the third estate had common reason to fear those sections of the nobility representing the forces of feudal reaction (Hampson, 1963, p.107).

The precise causes of the Revolution of 1789 in its specific timing were therefore complex. The role of the ideas of the philosophes was clearly an important one. However, the efforts and social effects of the different vested interests in response to their modernising ideas were far from predetermined. For example, it could be argued that a more determined and consistent attempt to modernise from above by Louis XVI may have carried the day. What is not in dispute is the fact that in their attack on clericism and the institutions of feudalism, the philosophes played a key role in unleashing social forces which went far beyond what they had advocated.

At the time the Revolution was felt to be an epoch making event in human history and subsequent theories which divide history into sequential stages have emphasised its magnitude. The Marxist account essentially viewed it as the explosion of pent up bourgeois power, heralding the emergence of capitalism from feudalism. However, industrial capitalism would be some time in emerging. The Comtian model emphasised the key role of the critical ideas of the philosophes in undermining the intellectual and moral foundations of the old order, which, when brought down by the Revolution, left in its wake a period of intellectual and social anarchy. According to Cobban (1974, Chs.2 & 14), such models would appear to be over-simplistic in their excessive reading of laws and stages into history. Additionally, more recent revisionist social historians such as McPhee (1992) and Price (1987) have recognised the existence of greater continuity across the Revolution, the latter arguing that more significant social and economic change was afoot during the middle of the nineteenth century under Louis Napoleon.

Viewed from the height of the Revolution in 1793-1794, the revisionist emphasis might appear to be implausible. The government had been forced by circumstances over which it had little control to radicalize the Revolution. Louis XVI had been executed and royal absolutism had long since crumbled. Those sections of the nobility most hostile to the Revolution had largely escaped to become émigrés. Their lands were nationalized and some sold. Areas of church land met a similar fate. The clergy had been required to sign a Civil Constitution and church property was desecrated during a period of dechristianization (Hampson, 1963, pp.198-206). Ceremonies commemorating the Revolution were held and as a symbol of monumental change, a new Revolutionary calendar was introduced. Universal suffrage was brought in, the ceremonial content of marriage reduced and divorce was legalised.

Meanwhile, émigré enemies of the Revolution were lining up with foreign powers preparing to invade and re-impose the ancien regime. Internally, the urban sans-culottes aimed to further proletarianize the Revolution (Hampson, 1963, Ch.VIII). A general atmosphere of fear and paranoia reigned as the doctrines of the philosophes were selectively appropriated to suit the perceived contingencies of desperate situations (Hampson, 1963, pp.217-225). From a position of Revolutionary decentralization, democracy, chaos and vulnerability, the Revolution lurched into the Reign of Terror with Robespierre falling back on the doctrine of Rousseau and imposing a dictatorship in the name of the 'general will' during a time of national emergency (Salvemini, 1963, p.297).

Moderation could only return when the forces of reaction and further revolution were suppressed. This was largely accomplished in 1795. The efforts of émigré and foreign armies to invade and turn back the clock ended in debacle (Salvemini, 1963, pp.319-324). This left the government free to crush the remaining radical force – the urban sans-culottes – who were unsupported by the peasantry for whom the Revolution had achieved its main aims.

The Revolution had now run its radical course. It had swept away the privileges and burdens of an estate system. The nobility and upper echelons of the clergy had lost lands and tax exemptions. Bourgeois speculators were the main beneficiaries in the sale of acquired lands (Dupeux, 1976, pp.105-118). To the peasantry, the redistribution of land was not great and mainly comprised the acquisition of mortgaged smallholdings. McPhee (1992, Ch.5) has calculated that peasant holdings comprised 33% of land prior to the Revolution and had only increased to 40% shortly after. The main benefit was clearer title of ownership and greater freedom of use (Dupeux, 1976, pp.105-106). Income from land and property sales had provided the government with much needed revenue. It had also consolidated the support of the beneficiaries to the defence of a new social order. The question was, what sort of social and political order would emerge?

Despite the freedoms and gains which the Revolution had brought to various parties of the third estate, for decades after a feeling of loss was commonly experienced. This was not primarily the material loss experienced by some, but in particular it bore a connection to the new freedoms. Despite the eventual imposition of order under Napoleon Bonaparte, society exhibited an abnormal lack of moral cohesion. In this context, we can distinguish two contrary but related analyses. The first especially reflected the position of those most privileged under the old regime; the hope for a return to the security, certainties and dogma of the old social order. This position was most clearly represented by the émigré nobles de Bonald and de Maistre who desired the full restoration of feudalism and Catholicism.

For de Bonald and de Maistre, the social consequences of the Enlightenment writings had been the erosion of faith in the infallibility of the teachings of the Catholic Church. This undermined faith in the divinely appointed organic social order and encouraged man to attempt to re-order society on rational principles. But, they argued, it is up to God in his infinite wisdom to order society, and it is for the good of man to have faith in God and know that his way is the best. Any attempt by man to change society by his own limited power of reason will not maximise happiness but instead, as in the case of the French Revolution and its aftermath, inevitably increase human misery. Man's assertion of his free will in this way was seen as interfering with the course of divine providence – much to his sufferings – and, it was argued, disproves the atheistic arrogant and evil ideals of the philosophes when confronted with the practical problem of social reconstruction (Lively, 1965). Mankind is essentially of imperfect nature and irrational impulses which require control through a social hierarchy and institutions vested in mystery. The only beneficial course for man to take in post-Revolution France was thus to re-establish faith in the divine providence of God and return to a feudal Catholic society where knowledge is based on faith and tradition (Zeitlin, 1968, Ch.5).

The second approach was more forward looking and rationalist in its emphasis. Saint Simon and Comte argued the need for a new social doctrine appropriate to the emerging new social type to act as the intellectual and moral basis for the re-establishment of social cohesion. The new social and moral order had to be scientifically anticipated. This was only possible through the application of rational analysis to the study of history with the purpose of identifying laws of social progress. It will be shown that for these theorists, the laws that they extrapolated from their reading of history pointed to the imminent emergence of a relatively meritocratic and centrally regulated industrial society.

With a degree of social stability established, a constitutional government referred to as the 'Directory' was formed in 1795. Adopting an increasingly dictatorial response in the face of famine, inflation and a pro-royalist uprising, it became replaced by a more effective dictatorship under Napoleon Bonaparte from 1799. This regime offered some hope to the proponents of both outlooks. The Revolution has broken centralization from the old regime. Under Napoleon, the centralized state was rebuilt and social order re-imposed by combining the gains of the Revolution with elements of the pre-Revolution heritage. Legal codification established uniform rights and duties. Under the appearance of democratic institutions, society became regimented and organised toward military efficiency. Education was opened up more to talent. Higher educational institutions, such as the Ecole Polytechnic which had been established in 1794, were geared to the application of science, but within a regimented educational system which opposed free thinking and directed talent toward military purposes (Dickinson, 1927, Ch.2). A new service nobility was instituted, ennobling top military men and civil servants. Émigrés were pardoned and allowed to return, some managing to reclaim unsold lands. Catholicism was again officially recognized, but now as the 'majority religion' rather than the state religion.

Following the military defeat of Napoleon, the victorious powers imposed a constitutional monarchy. At this juncture in French history, there existed a precarious balance of opposing social and political forces in a society in which constitutional monarchy had no tradition (Dickinson, 1927, Ch.3; Wright, 1981, Ch.9). More émigrés returned in the hope of a full counter-revolution comprising a restoration of their titles, privileges and lost lands, and the re-establishment of the Catholic Church to a position of past religious and moral ascendancy. They found some of the signs encouraging. Unsold nationalized lands were reclaimed. Religious campaigning became more active and divorce was made unavailable from 1816. The suffrage was considerably contracted through property qualification requirements. But as the monarchy showed further reactionary intent during the late 1820s, beneficiaries of the Revolution, orchestrated by bourgeois elements, made common cause in the overthrow of the Bourbons in the Revolution of 1830.

The constitutional monarchy of Louis Philippe which took the helm now reflected the sectional interests of a narrow bourgeois elite. With the threat of counter-revolution passed, the government turned its attention to the suppression of strikes and rioting by workers whose expectations of more far reaching reform had been dashed and whose conditions were deteriorating. The most notorious of strikes was the uprising of Lyon silk workers, but the regime had suppressed such outbreaks by 1834. Against this background, there were appearing a number of utopian schemes for the reorganisation of society which substituted co-operation for competition. Such schemes included those proposed by followers of Saint Simon, the Saint Simonians, as well as those of Fourier, Cabet, Blanc, Blanqui and Proudhon.

'Enrich yourselves' were the catchwords of the regime, but industrial modernization based on enterprise culture between 1830 and 1848 was limited. A relatively large proportion of the population still lived an isolated and primitive subsistence life on agricultural smallholdings and small workshops were typical size businesses (Wolf, 1963, Ch.4). In time honoured French tradition, those who had 'enriched themselves' through business enterprise often searched for social status in the purchase of a country chateau, and the regime instituted a nobility of the bourgeoisie.

By 1848, the bourgeois monarchy had alienated all but a small social stratum. It was opposed by legitimists and despised by downtrodden workers, and collapsed when it lost the support of the largely petty-bourgeois National Guard (Wolf, 1963, Ch.5). The Catholic Church was initially sympathetic to the revolutionary overthrow of a regime whose liberal economic reforms had inflicted injustices on workers. However, the Revolution aroused fears amongst the propertied classes of a socialist threat to property. They were prepared to turn to the party of order, soon to be supported by the church, to terminate the disorders.

Louis Napoleon was elected to power in 1848, remained in power through a coup in 1851 and became emperor in 1852. He instituted a populist regime which retained power until 1870. The exact nature of Louis Napoleon's rule has been a matter of much dispute. Many writers have emphasised the authoritarian nature of the regime and its manipulation of right wing populist support, especially from that of the lower middle classes and the peasantry. Schapiro (1948, Ch.13) has even characterised the regime as an early model of fascism. According to this analysis, Louis Napoleon manipulated a counterfeit democracy; he used the plebiscite to draw the sting of revolutionary pressures and manipulated the outcomes through the dictatorship that the plebiscite legitimised. Others, for example Green (1965, Ch.5), have minimized the repressiveness of the regime and emphasised its genuine concern for the welfare of workers. Less in dispute has been the fact that this regime established French industrial take-off through state intervention in the form of subsidies for private enterprise and credit banking geared toward the needs of large scale capital projects such as city development and railway construction. The establishment of limited liability companies also encouraged private investment into large scale businesses.

Overall, French modernization from the Revolution of 1789 through to industrialization was remarkable for the social upheavals which replaced one type of regime with another. However, although society frequently lurched between the extremes of revolution and reaction, France remained characterised by certain quite deep rooted traditions. Despite the values of liberty expressed in the Revolution, French history was characterised by continuity in state centralisation from royal absolutism, to Napoleonic rule, to a lesser extent in the regime of Louis Philippe and then again in the regime of Louis Napoleon. Despite efforts by Louis Philippe, it was very difficult for entrepreneurship working within the context of a free market to strongly emerge and when industrialisation did arrive it was of state induced form. As well as the utopian thinking of the philosophes, France was also marked by utopian co-operative schemes and strong currents of left and right wing populism (something which is seen to this day) which Louis Napoleon managed to harness during his period of rule.

Despite the fierce attacks launched by the philosophes and the Revolution, Catholicism remained a potent force which the propertied classes were keen to fall back on to help establish order after upheaval and despite the subsequent triumph of a secular republican state, the influence of Catholicism in France has been enduring. Again, despite the 1789 Revolution and its successors, France's vibrant feudal heritage saw both traditional and new nobilities wielding considerable influence and members of the middle class intent on imitating a noble lifestyle. Saint Simon's and Comte's theories of progress attempted to explain social instability but also reflected such French traditions.

One attempt to offer a broad contextualization of the French route to modernisation has been provided by Barrington More (1967), which related the nature of political institutions growing out of modernization to variations between societies in terms of the vibrancy of their feudal heritage. According to this analysis, in England, the early decline of feudalism and growing power of commercial interests assisted the pathway to the emergence of liberal democratic political institutions and a free market economy. By contrast, in countries such as Germany and Japan, a pervasive feudalism combined with modernisation forced from above provided a pathway toward fascist totalitarianism. For Barrington Moore, the profile of French modernisation provided an intermediate route between these two positions. Its feudal heritage was more entrenched and royal absolutism more pronounced than had been the case in England, limiting its capacity to modernise through commercial free market activity. Furthermore, it combined revolutions from below with interventionist modernisation from above.

2 | **Henri Saint Simon**

Saint Simon was convinced that post–Revolution France remained in an unstable social and political condition, the remedy of which required the realisation of a social order different to that of the past. He argued that the analysis of history to reveal laws of change was a prerequisite to establishing a model of the form that the new social order will take. This task he embarked upon, yet his own analysis of history was usually sketchy and his schemes for social reconstruction varied. His works were the output of an enlightened noble and opportunist searching for recognition, finance and influence with various post-Revolution elites. They combined Restorationist and Enlightenment influences. To appreciate these influences, it is necessary to start with a brief biographical outline.

Saint Simon: enlightened noble and opportunist

Born in Paris in 1760, Saint Simon was of that generation who grew up in the cauldron of Enlightenment discussion, lived through the turmoil of the Revolution and was distanced from the brutality of feudalism. He was great-nephew of the Duke de Saint Simon, a reactionary court noble to Louis XIV, and claimed to have traced his lineage back to Charlemagne (Ionescu, 1976, p.13; Markham, 1952, p.Xi). Yet he also made the dubious claim, only supported in his own 'Memoires', to have been briefly tutored during his youth by the Encyclopaedist d'Alembert (Manuel, 1965, p.13) and was apparently imprisoned by his father for his refusal to take communion (Sokoloff, 1975, p.34). Saint Simon was strong willed and always convinced that he had great things to achieve. The energy and optimism of this mercurial character led to a life rich in practical exploits and proposals for grand construction projects. Later in life, driven by naïve optimism and an overinflated sense of self-importance, Saint Simon believed that his mission as a social philosopher was to provide an urgently needed plan for social reconstruction. There is therefore often a messianic tone to his works.

Whilst still in his teens, Saint Simon was active as a career officer fighting the British in the American War of Independence, seeing action as a captain in the French army at the age of nineteen (Markham, 1952, p.Xi; Manuel, 1965, pp.14-15). He was not animated in his duties by ideals of freedom or justice. However, on the North American continent Saint Simon grasped the image of an industrious and relatively open society free from the inherited idleness and servitude of feudalism (Normano, 1933, pp. 8-14; Gray, 1946, Ch.6). This image helped to form his highly perceptive view of the need for European regeneration in the post-feudal industrial society.

Saint Simon was widely travelled. As well as America he visited Mexico, Switzerland, Germany, England, Holland and Spain. His cosmopolitan outlook led to a recognition of the importance of international transport systems, especially canal projects, as the key to growing industrialization.

Some members of Saint Simon's family opposed the French Revolution and became émigrés. However, Saint Simon pragmatically and opportunistically followed the Revolutionary tide. He became representative of his local commune, but played no substantial part in the Revolution. During this period he dropped his aristocratic title of Count Henri Claude de Rouvray de Saint Simon and renamed himself 'Henri Bonhomme'. In a business partnership with Count Redern, who supplied most of the finance but later liquidated the partnership (Markham, 1952, pp. Xii-XiV; Manuel, 1965, pp.106-107), he made a fortune through speculation in old hotels and properties of émigré landlords as well as abbeys and ex-church lands. These were purchased with small down payments, the balance to be paid at a later date in a currency that was quickly depreciating due to the effects of inflation (Markham, 1952, pp.Xii-XiV).

Saint Simon was imprisoned in November 1793 during one of Robespierre's round ups of suspect subversives (Sokoloff, 1975, pp.24-28; Manuel, 1965, p.27), possibly in a case of mistaken identity of a wanted Belgian banker, Henry Simon. It has been suggested that Saint Simon's property dealings under the cover of pseudonyms may have aroused the suspicions of the authorities (Markham, 1952, pp. Xii-Xiii). Hearing of his imprisonment, locals petitioned his good character and he was eventually released in October 1794.

Whilst in prison, Saint Simon claimed to have experienced a visitation from his supposed distant ancestor Charlemagne, revealing to him his future role as a first rate philosopher (Sokoloff, 1975, pp. 24-25)! Only from 1798 did Saint Simon begin to apply himself to social philosophy.

Animated by a sense of urgent mission to terminate what he regarded to be a state of intellectual and moral chaos in post-Revolutionary France, he was convinced that his role as a social philosopher would assist this accomplishment. Saint Simon felt that through applying a scientific approach to the study of history, a direction of social change could be established from which could be projected the form that an immanent new social order would take.

Yet he seemed educationally ill prepared for such a task. He had no formal scientific training, and both his knowledge of science and his proposals for social reconstruction turned out to be quite superficial and naïve. Saint Simon's knowledge of history was sketchy and in post-Revolution France the subject was little and poorly taught (Hayek, 1952, Pt.2, Ch.1). However, his finances at this time were still buoyant. In 1797 he had moved near to the Ecole Polytechnique, the prestigious educational establishment for the applied sciences. He lavished part of his fortune on inviting leading scientists to banquets as a means of gleaning in conversation the latest ideas in the various fields of science (Hayek, 1952, pp. 118-119). This procedure was repeated when he moved close to the Ecole de Medicine, and this strategy helps to explain his acquisition of a feel for science and his intuitive type vision of the outlines of a future industrial order.

Meanwhile, he visited England and Germany and at the former was much influenced by utilitarianism and its emphasis on the maximization of human happiness – an outlook characteristic of the Enlightenment and already expounded by leading philosophes in France.

Saint Simon duly turned to writing at the relatively late age of forty-two, his first work entitled Letters from an Inhabitant of Geneva to his Contemporaries (translations are included in Markham, 1952; Ionescu, 1976; and Taylor, 1975) improvising his social philosophy from his colourful worldly experiences and the ideas of his academic guests. From this point on, he toyed with variations on his general scheme for social reconstruction as he attempted to ingratiate himself with various elites and became increasingly desperate for the recognition of his ideas. Saint Simon initially proposed a new social order which would be organised by the most able scientists, proposing a Council of Newton to be headed by Napoleon Bonaparte. Sending out copies of his early works, he first appealed to Napoleon himself as well as leading ministers and scientists (Manuel, 1965, pp. 109-110), but was largely ignored as a nuisance. By 1805, his money had been used up. He was temporarily rescued from his plight by the financial support of a previous servant who had since made good, but spent much of the remainder of his life in extreme poverty, needing to beg for assistance. During 1812-1813, with war raging and in great despondency over his poverty and lack of recognition, Saint Simon suffered a psychic breakdown and was institutionalized in the lunatic asylum at Charenton.

Saint Simon's recovery came with international peace and Bourbon Restoration. In his 'Constitutional Proposals to the King' (Taylor, 1975, Extract 29), Saint Simon expressed his support for the Restoration monarchy so long as it sided with the modernizing forces of industry. In disgust for the scientists' lack of vision to fulfil their historic role as leaders of a new industrial order which would be geared toward peaceful productivity, he relegated scientists from the position of social pre-eminence in the new social order that they had occupied in his earlier works. In pursuit of recognition and finance, Saint Simon retuned his scheme of social rebuilding by raising the status of industrialists in the new order and acting as their propagandist in his journal L' Industrie which was launched in 1816 (Iggers, 1958, pp.12-15). During this phase of his writings, Saint Simon temporarily voiced the virtues of liberal economics and his admiration of the British constitution (Markham, 1952, pp.28-64; Manuel, 1963, Ch.14), briefly believing that he had found his ultimate science for social reconstruction in the ideas of the political economists (Hewett, p.4, 19/1/2015). He soon emphasised, however, an important distinction between political and administrative institutions, only the latter of which he advocated as fully in tune with the needs of the emerging industrial society. His alliance with the liberal economists was therefore short lived. In following his tendency to advocate a more centrally regulated society, Saint Simon became critical of the ideas of the political economists and of free market industrialisation as a system that benefited only a minority and abandoned the poor. His financial support from industrialists unsurprisingly evaporated.

The following years, whilst never abandoning efforts to court industrialists, witnessed the publication of a series of other journals in which he (although the articles were sometimes penned by his new secretary Auguste Comte) indicted all current political power holders as idlers and criticised scientists for continuing to work as specialists rather than providing the socially necessary function of developing science as a coherent body of integrated ideas.

In his final years, Saint Simon's attention switched to the need to ameliorate the plight of the poor. He emphasised the need for a new religious morality of brotherhood as the basis for social order, harmony and maximum happiness, this leading to the publication of 'The New Christianity' in 1825. In another bout of despair, in 1823, just two years before he died in Paris, he made an unsuccessful attempt at suicide by shooting himself in the head. Upon recovery, he was assisted by a small gathering of followers and principally the finance of a Portugese Jewish banker, Olinde Rodrigues, to live his last years free from desperate poverty.

Saint Simon's view of history: the progress of enlightenment or the progress of dogma?

For Ionescu (1976, Introduction), Saint Simon's view of history exhibited a strong strand of ontological idealism; what essentially determined the condition of society was the condition of the prevailing system of ideas, of which society was the application. As Saint Simon put it:

> 'every social regime is an application of a philosophic system.....
> consequently, it is impossible to institute a new regime, without
> having first established the new philosophical system to which it
> should correspond' (L'Industrie, 1817, quoted in Manuel, 1963,
> p.233).

The key to understanding the history of social change thus resided in an analysis of changes in prevailing world views.

Historical progress, Saint Simon claimed, could be measured by the progress of science which enabled man to exploit his environment with increasing efficiency. There is clearly a powerful Enlightenment influence here. However, social cohesion required science to be in the safe hands of a spiritual elite. For Saint Simon, there was no essential contradiction between the advance of science and the persistence of religion. From his elitist viewpoint, religion was simply the allegorical expression of the state of science by the relatively enlightened spiritual elite, conveyed in the form of a dogma to provide an integrated belief system to bond the ignorant masses to the social order.

Saint Simon viewed social history from a high vantage point as a massive moving process of alternating 'organic' and 'critical' phases. Organic phases were durable and extended stages in history where unified systems of thinking prevailed and society existed in an integrated state. This was seen by Saint Simon as a benign social condition. Critical phases comprised temporary and transitional stages, providing the means of change between different types of organic society. Characteristic of critical phases would be the breakdown of unified belief systems and social order. All societies in history, whatever their specific regime and whether during organic or critical phases, could be bracketed as 'militant', since they were all characterised by the political suppression of the productive by the idle. Contrasted to militant societies is the 'industrial' type. In this type of society, all members work productively and power politics is superseded by the administration of production, itself a productive activity. Saint Simon claimed that his study of history revealed a direction of social change through which: 1) French society had entered a critical state, heightened by the ideas of the philosophes who had attacked the world view of feudalism, culminating in the Revolution; 2) that a new organic period was on the horizon and 3) that this new society, the industrial society, would be fundamentally different from all others in history.

Saint Simon saw the feudal society of the eleventh century as a highly integrated social organism. Social cohesion rested on the spiritual authority of a pervasive Catholicism, which demanded unquestioning faith, and the repressive temporal authority of the nobility. The ignorance and coarseness of the masses required these constraints. The church was at the forefront of science and education, translating the limited scientific knowledge into palatable religious truths for the masses, and the Papacy promoted harmony between nations – a highly romanticised view of the past in which Saint Simon was influenced by the works of de Bonald.

To Saint Simon, the organic cohesion of feudal society and international harmony started to become undermined when the church came to preoccupy itself in serving the sectional interests of the political (temporal) powers (Taylor, 1975, Extract 40, The New Christianity). He argued that the social organism of feudalism was becoming weakened as the Catholic Church distorted the true Christian message of brotherly love to ally itself with the political repression of the masses by the idle nobility. Through this corrupting liaison, the church became obstructionist to the progress of science which was consequently falling into the hands of laymen. The role of laymen in the advance of science came to undermine the spiritual authority of the church and the social cohesion which rested on it. Internationally, the harmony of Papal spiritual rule was giving way to conflicts between political powers.

Saint Simon argued that those societies in which Protestantism was making the greatest headway were experiencing social dissipation as religion demanding blind faith in the teachings of the church hierarchy was losing ground to a religion which freed the examination of religious matters to the conscience of the individual.

France had been relatively resistant to the influence of Protestantism, but the attack on Catholicism and feudal privilege later gathered force in the critical ideas of the Enlightenment philosophes (Brumfitt, 1972, Chs. 6 & 7; Mornet, 1969, Pt, 3, Ch. 3). According to Saint Simon, by the 1750s France had entered a critical phase of breakdown which was transitional between a once organic phase of feudalism and the emergence of a new organic era in the form of the industrial society of the immanent future. The French Revolution represented the height of this breakdown. The post-Revolution experience of loss and continuing social and political destabilisation was the product of intellectual turmoil and break from the past, prior to the necessary emergence of a new social order headed by a new spiritual elite who would replace the clergy and convey a dogma appropriate to reconstruction in the new age of advanced science and industry.

For Bury (1920, Ch. XIV), this analysis reflected the sobering effect which the experience of the social destabilisation of the Revolution had on Saint Simon's (and Comte's) attitude toward the philosophes. Whilst greatly influenced by their progressivism, Saint Simon did not share their personal aversion toward religion or their faith in an analytic approach to science as the basis for social progress. Furthermore, he held a less disparaging view of the church and religion under the feudal order. Having suffered the intellectual attacks of rationalists and those on its institutions during the Revolution, its place will need to be taken by a new form of religion which promoted a holistic outlook and integrated body of values which were appropriate to the industrial society and advanced stage of science which was necessary for rebuilding social order. The position of advocates of a return to the old regime, as personified by de Bonald and de Maistre, was also therefore untenable since it required the abandonment of reason in the search to reassert order on the basis of irrationality and blind faith in supernatural forces. Centuries of the development of science and the emergence of faith in progress could not be reversed. In his solution, Saint Simon attuned the organicism of the counter-Revolutionary writers to the requirements of post-Revolutionary society by turning it to the future and orientating religion to a this-worldly emphasis. Progress meant that religion, which had emphasised the fall of man and the need for his repression, and which had become anti-science, needed to be superseded by religion as the worship of science, the source of improving man's lot on earth.

In the industrial society, the masses, immersed in their productive capacities, would always need science to be mediated to them in the form of religion. To re-establish social cohesion, a new spiritual scientific elite, at once regulating society through the science of social physics and inculcating the cult of science to the masses in the form of an organised belief system, must emerge to replace the Catholic priesthood. The social utility of religion, Saint Simon posited, would thus remain attuned to the ignorance of the masses through the conversion of the current state of science to that of a cohesive dogma in the hands of a new elite who were up to the mark with science to promote social cohesion. In this way, science would revert from the destructive role of critical analysis which precipitated the Revolution, to a socially constructive synthesising approach. However, in his last major work, New Christianity, Saint Simon came to view the religion of science as insufficient for promoting the moral basis for social cohesion in the industrial society and emphasised the need for altruism in the form of brotherly love in human relationships to bind individuals to society.

Positivism and social progress toward the industrial society

The nature of the new emerging social type and the inevitability of social progress toward it found its basis in Saint Simon's positivism. Society, like all phenomena, claimed Saint Simon, operated according to natural laws. But how could this view be justified? An overview of history, according to Saint Simon, showed the spread of the scientific outlook from the inorganic to the organic sciences – an insight obtained from the works of Burdin and later systematized by Comte in his hierarchy of the sciences. Society was regarded as the highest form of organism. The effect of the advance of science on society had initially been to undermine religion and, given Saint Simon's idealism, with it the cohesion of the social organism. In cataloguing the achievements of science in the Encyclopaedia, the philosophes had launched an attack on religion (Brumfitt, 1972, pp. 138-146). For Saint Simon, because this approach to science remained fragmented, analytical and critical, its effect was socially destructive. It maligned much that could be commended from the past without yet advancing to the mature stage of providing an integrated and constructive understanding of the social realm for purposes of rebuilding. Saint Simon maintained that social reconstruction required the establishment of the final synthesised science of 'social physics'. This would enable a new scientific elite to understand and terminate the critical condition of the social present. By taking power, they would use social physics to provide the constructive element to foreshorten social destabilisation and inaugurate the industrial society. Science and religion would again become reconciled; religion needed to become this worldly and science social and synthesised. With the spread of science to an understanding of all realms of phenomena including the social, the ultimate synthesis of knowledge and highest level of social cohesion would be grounded in a new coherent philosophy (Manuel, 1963, Ch.10).

Further than this, Saint Simon adopted a 'monist' position. To give order throughout the sciences, he was searching for a unifying principle applicable to the scientific understanding of the physical, biological and social world (Manuel, 1963, Ch. 8). In Letters from an Inhabitant of Geneva to his Contemporaries, he speculated on the concept of gravitation for this purpose. Although he left it vague, this would establish the grounding of the fledgling science of society on the central concept of what he saw as Newton's proven science of planetary motion.

How might this principle be detected in Saint Simon's social theory? It could be argued that for Saint Simon, social cohesion derives from a cohesive world view which acts like a social centre of gravity and that social change follows a gravitational type pull to the future along a pre-determined unilinear path. Thus, at the height of feudalism, Catholicism was the prevailing world view making for social unity and the Papacy acted as a central force promoting community amongst nations. The advance of the Reformation, of scientific reasoning, and of the Enlightenment all progressively weakened this centre of gravity and precipitated the collapse of the feudal structure, as well as bringing shifting alliances and political hostilities between militant nations. To Saint Simon, in post-Revolution France, only repressive government such as that instituted by Napoleon Bonaparte could hold society together whilst this condition remained. However, this could not be a natural long term solution. For political repression to abate, a new organic era had to emerge. This social type would be organised for the benefit of all producers by elites of the most able scientists and industrialists – although the predominance of one group or the other changed with Saint Simon's schemes. But science and industry would also require religious significance for the masses if society were to cohere. Referring to the new secular religion which Saint Simon anticipated, Durkheim later commented that:

'It is against this tendency toward dispersion that religion must react. It should again show man that the world – in spite of its diversity – is a phenomena leading them back to God. Thus it has a role no different from that of philosophy. Religion does not require a celestial image opposed to the earthly ones. Its true mission is not to turn mankind away from temporal reality in order to bind it to some supra-experimental object, but simply to emphasise the unity of reality' (Durkheim, 1959, pp. 182-183).

In Saint Simon's scheme, human understanding of social change had itself progressed with the advance of science. Thus, under Catholicism, social change was viewed as the mysterious outcome of divine providence. The development of science, in attacking religion, first critically undermined this fatalistic notion. Its ultimate positive role was in revealing the laws of social change. As a result, social prediction became possible and the outlines of the future social order could be established with scientific certainty. Science thus substituted for fatalism knowledge of unilinear social progress in which man could play an active part in social reconstruction. It provided a foundation to foreshorten the pains of the transitional period of social destabilization through foreknowledge of the form that the emerging society will take.

In Letters from an Inhabitant of Geneva to his Contemporaries (Ionescu, 1976, pp. 65-70), Saint Simon personified the outlook of man during the course of social progress. Prior to the Enlightenment, man was characterised as walking backwards along a pre-set path to the future with his gaze fixed on the past and knowing little of where he was going. He may have been trying to walk in the direction that he was facing, toward a 'golden past'. Such was the posture of the 'ancients'.

The great benefit of the Enlightenment was that man started to turn his gaze from the past to the future. Following the Revolution, part of society became intent on turning back to restore the past, and part turned fully round to see the future in all of its clarity. Saint Simon was confident that he had provided a vision of that society to be embraced by progressivists. But, he argued, whatever man's preference, he was impelled to walk in the direction of progress to the industrial society of the 'golden future' for which he could prepare himself and ease his stride by adopting the latter outlook.

Although argued to be the logical outcome of laws of social change, the precise nature of Saint Simon's industrial society varied in relation to the different modernising elites that he was pragmatically, even opportunistically, at pains to gain recognition and support from. It is therefore problematic to summarise his 'model' of the industrial society. Generally, his industrial typology agreed with that of the political economists on two significant points: firstly, the predominating importance of industry, especially when interpreted broadly as industriousness, and secondly the decline of political intervention.

But there were significant contrasts. For the political economists, social integration could emerge spontaneously from the pursuit of individual interests within the private enterprise free market system with minimal government intervention. Production could be best enhanced by responsiveness to consumer demand and the release of industry from external regulation. Whilst Saint Simon was temporarily (around 1814-1815) attracted to the ideas of political economy as the potential new science, he came to adopt the position that such an accumulation of individual interests was an insufficient basis for the social cohesion of the new organic era. Furthermore, he argued that industrial potential could best be enhanced through a form of control that he viewed as post-political. To Saint Simon, all throughout history, political regimes were characterised by the manipulation of the productive poor by the idle rich. Such regimes were divisive and would be unnecessary in the industrial society in which both administrative elites, as technocratic planners, and workers, who would elect them, would commonly play productive roles (Ionescu, 1976, pp.29-42). As knowledge of the social realm became scientific, leading scientists and industrialists would take the helm on merit. The destructive preoccupation with power politics and factional interests would give way to the productive activity of the efficient regulation of production for the broader social well-being.

In these respects, Saint Simon contrasted the industrial society with the repressive regimes and wasteful conflicts of interest of the militant age. However, in his image of the industrial society, Saint Simon's sympathetic portrayal of the feudal past as well as the French tradition of centralization shone through. In the spiritual sphere, social scientists should rise to their destiny and, replacing the clergy, assisted by artists, adopt an ideological role of promoting the cult of science (or later the New Christianity of altruism) to the masses as the established religion. In the temporal sphere, and of varying relative importance to scientists dependent on the scheme proposed, the social hierarchy would be headed by an industrial elite who would replace the idle feudal nobility. With Newtonian type clockwork precision, the elites would apply their scientific and industrial understanding to regulate society as a massive efficient industrial enterprise. Science and industry offered the prospect of a new national and international order of peaceful coexistence superior even to that which he claimed was achieved by Catholicism during the height of feudalism and in which the exploitation of the productive by the idle would be replaced by the application of science and new productive forces in the common exploitation of nature. What is less clear is by what means, other than the overwhelming climate of moral opinion associated with a new intellectual era, privileged owners of productive property were expected to relinquish their political power to specialist administrators? Moreover, even if such a transition were possible, what guarantees would there be that administration, far from superseding politics, would not take the form of totalitarianism?

Science, utopia and totalitarianism
Liberal theorists have been strong critics of the method and implications of the positivist notion of historical laws. Simon (1956) has argued that Saint Simon's interpretation of history was subject to his utopian image of the future. On the assumption rather than the demonstration of the operation of social laws, Saint Simon took a selective high altitude sketch which carved history into a series of alternating organic (stable) and critical (unstable) stages. Feudalism was favourably characterised as a

period of social harmony and integration. Following a phase of social disintegration, social laws indicated the inevitable emergence of a higher organic stage in the industrial society. For Simon, this appeal to scientific laws of change allied with a selective view of history was in scientific terms premature. Furthermore, it enabled Saint Simon to convert his hope of utopia into certainty and justified intervention to smooth the path of change to what would effectively be a totalitarian order.

The free market liberal Hayek (1952) has maintained that it is not possible to know the detailed workings of a society where people are free to make their own subjective decisions; certainly not in terms of physical laws. He has used the term 'scientism' to refer to attempts to overextend science and the misapplication of the outlook of the physical sciences to the social sphere. For Hayek, in attempting such a misapplication, Saint Simon's positivism claimed to apprehend the law like operation of social wholes which it took to know better than the minute detail of the parts. Whilst Saint Simon used the appeal of science to substantiate his vision of the new order, his own approach was not scientific. Historical detail was ignored as a shortcut to grasping social wholes in history intuitively, thereby disregarding the precise empirical data upon which positivist science was supposedly based. The outcome was that the desire to impose a blueprint for social intervention to fit a utopian model took precedence – for Hayek, resulting in a totalitarian monstrosity which would be imposed in the guise of science.

Social theory which makes large scale social prophecies with reference to scientific laws of historical forces has been referred to by Popper (1974) as pro-naturalistic historicism. It bases a prophesied social reconfiguration on the apparent certainty of social laws derived from apprehending social wholes in the course of history. For Popper, an empirical base for social science can only be soundly established slowly through the feedback process of small scale social experiments. Knowledge of social wholes can only be very selective. Basing laws of change on such a selective process is regarded as pre-scientific and the image of the future a utopian construct. Although emphasising progress, historicists are highly conservative. Being afraid of uncertain change, they need to eliminate uncertainty through belief in laws of change which we cannot know exist but which they then attempt to impose. Social theorists adopting such a position portray an intellectual megalomania and their schemes a propensity for the imposition of totalitarian institutions.

Despite claiming scientific certainty in his analysis, Saint Simon's schemes for social reconstruction varied. He first favoured a scientific elite and appealed to Napoleon. Exasperated that under Napoleon scientists were subverting the course of history by applying science to warfare, he later courted an industrial elite and what he hoped to be an enlightened Bourbon monarchy to institute his industrial society. Again contemptuously ignored by the political regime, he finally argued the need to re-establish the essential Christian message of 'brotherly love' as the altruistic basis for social cohesion and concern for the plight of the poor during a period of Catholic revivalism in France as the monarchy took a more ultra turn.

The Saint Simonians and Saint Simonism
Saint Simon died in 1825. A small group of followers, the Saint Simonians, claiming privileged insight into his thinking, developed Saint Simon's ideas further in a religions, interventionist and authoritarian direction (Iggers, 1958). They took up Saint Simon's distinction between organic and critical social periods but made less use of the militant and industrial typology. By their definition, religion prevailed during organic periods, and critical periods, characterised by social strife and factionalism, were irreligious phases. Catholicism had been the religion of the last organic period. It was undermined by the religious criticisms of the Reformation and the irreligion of the Enlightenment. By the 1830s, liberal economic doctrines, parliamentary democracy and analytic science were features of the current critical phase. In France, the Revolution of 1830 had simply completed the Revolution of 1789 and established the ascendency of a small bourgeois elite. This phase needed to be terminated for the higher organic period to emerge in the industrial society.

The severity of their attack on liberal institutions distinguished the Saint Simonians from the outlook of Saint Simon. They recognized signs of industrialization under the regime of Louis Philippe, but Saint Simon's industrial society, integrated in the industriousness of both the regulators and regulated, had not arrived. Instead, industry had become deregulated and, they argued, owned and controlled by an idle capitalist class exploiting productive workers. Divisiveness, protests and political repression therefore remained (Iggers, 1958, Ch. 4).

Saint Simon had recognised that a natural diversity of talent existed across society and he provided an image of an industrial society which would be regulated by the most able as opposed to the feudal social hierarchy where political power derived from fortune of birth. But he was no egalitarian, and since for Saint Simon the emerging society would be essentially industrial, he did not directly confront the inherent contradiction between a meritocratic social hierarchy and the inheritance of private productive property along with its associated power advantages and privileges. In their criticism of the regime of the Bourgeois Monarchy, the

Saint Simonians did confront this contradiction. Their solution was a form of socialist industrial society.

In this industrial society, the utilisation of talent for the collective benefit would require the measurement of ability by experts as the means to the allocation of individuals to appropriate social roles (Iggers, 1958, Ch. 3). Abolishing the right of inheritance of productive private property, the state would direct its allocation on trust to those most capable of effectively utilizing it (Iggers, 1958, Ch. 6) and a central bank would encourage industrial projects through the administration of production funds to the capable.

Leaders would not be chosen by democratic process since the choice of superiors by inferiors would subvert the natural hierarchy of ability (Iggers, 1958, Ch.3). Instead, the leader would be recognized by his genius for actualizing the age to the masses. Through him, science and art would be directed for purposes of promoting social unanimity.

By the early 1830s, under the leadership of Bazard and Enfantin, Saint Simonism was becoming a mystical creed (Butler, 1926, Ch.2), contesting conventional bourgeois sexual morals by maintaining that inconstant sexual relationships were as acceptable as constant, since both were grounded in human nature. The cult's outlook was conveyed in pamphlets at highly charged public meetings. As a challenge to the moral outlook and vested interests of a bourgeois elite during a time of social unrest, the movement was charged with illegal assembly and their meeting places closed down. Leading members retreated to a monastic life in a country house at Melinmontant. They were subsequently charged with corruption of public morals and imprisoned. Ridicule, disbandment and collapse of public support soon followed (Butler, 1926, pp. 28-36).

When the period of industrial modernization arrived in France under Louis Napoleon, it followed an interventionist path through state subsidies and finance banking support for large scale capital projects. Leading Saint Simonians, who had returned to economic matters, emerged to play key roles as economists and in construction projects and finance banking (Butler, 1926, p.50; Iggers, 1958, pp. 36-37) and Louis Napoleon, attracted by Saint Simonian authoritarianism, cultivated the image of a Saint Simonian leader, a great leader who had captured the spirit of the times (Schapiro, 1948, Ch. 13).

3 | **Auguste Comte**

Born in Montpellier in January 1798, August Comte was of modest social background. His father was a straight laced and hard-working minor government official (Coser, 1977, pp.13-14). Comte's parents were both Catholic and royalist, but Comte was later to confess to his father that by the age of fourteen he had ceased to believe in God (Gould, 1920, p.3). Comte had benefited from the opening up of scientific education to talent under Napoleon Bonaparte and he became a committed republican. But as if in microcosm of the continuity amongst change in French modernization, we shall see that this apparent break from the traditionalist outlook of his parents was deceptive.

Comte: polytechnician and republican

At school during the Napoleonic era, Comte experienced military type discipline. He was an industrious student showing great ability in mathematics and the confidence to stand in for his mathematics teacher during his absence. At the age of sixteen, Comte won a place to study mathematics at the Ecole Polytechnic. Here he was aptly nicknamed the 'thinker'. But he did not complete his studies. Not for the last time, his assertiveness and arrogance were to cause him trouble. On one occasion, he rebuked a lecturer for his casual attitude to the class (Gould, 1920, pp.3-6). Then, identified as one of the ringleaders of student protest against the exam system, he was expelled in 1816 (Gould, 1920, p.7; Sokoloff, 1975, pp.59-60). Comte had built up a reputation for rebelliousness and when he was sent home in disgrace a police watch was kept on him (Sokoloff, 1975, p.60).

Comte soon returned to Paris and subsisted through conducting private lessons in mathematics (Gould, 1920, p.8). It was in Paris, during a period of economic depression, that as a youngster he expressed in a letter to a friend that he was affected by what he felt to be the immorality of a society which cast large numbers of people aside and into great poverty whilst others lived unconcerned in considerable wealth (Gould, 1920, pp.9-10). This was the 'freedom' won by the Revolution.

In Paris Comte met Saint Simon. He shared Saint Simon's view that post-Revolution French society remained in a period of unstable transition which required termination with the assistance of the discovery of laws of social change. Between 1817 and 1824, Comte worked as Saint Simon's secretary, drafting social and philosophical sketches for journals and pamphlets (Manuel, 1965, pp.251-260). Initially, he felt the liaison to be most beneficial, claiming in a letter to his friend Valat that under Saint Simon his thinking had progressed in six months as far as it might otherwise have done in three years (Durkheim, 1959, pp.106-107). Eventually, though, they parted in acrimonious circumstances.

Factors contributing to the rift included differing aptitudes, temperaments and social backgrounds. Saint Simon was a mercurial thinker, but certainly an intellectual inferior to Comte in terms of systematic theoretical thinking. Yet he maintained a condescending attitude toward his secretary and was more inclined to revise his schemes in the pursuit of personal gain, whereas for Comte social guidance required as a prerequisite carefully systematized social theory (Gould, 1920, p.10; Blumberg, p.iV in Martineau, 1855). Comte was not comfortable with Saint Simon's attempts to court the support of industrialists, the sketchiness of and modifications to his schemes for the new social order, or the turn of his later works toward religion. He became frustrated that his own essays were not gaining him sufficient recognition, often being published under Saint Simon's name. He saw his 1822 essay Plan for the Scientific Operations Necessary for Reorganizing Society (In Fletcher, 1974) as a personal intellectual milestone. According to Manuel's research, the crucial argument between them was triggered when this essay appeared in a publication by Saint Simon in 1824, implying that it was Saint Simon's work (Manuel, 1965, pp.252-259), along with a condescending introduction by Saint Simon stating his disagreement with some of Comte's ideas (Hewitt, 19/1/2015, p.7; Gould, 1920, p.18). Dispatched by Saint Simon, Comte never forgave him for what he felt to be very shoddy treatment (Manuel, 1965, pp.254-255). Almost thirty years later, in the preface to volume 3 of his System of Positive Polity (1875, pp.Xviii-XiX), Comte commented that 'I own nothing to that personage, not even the smallest instruction' and referred to Saint Simon as a 'depraved charlatan', a buyer and seller of ideas who did not have a single original thought.

In 1825 Comte married Caroline Massin, a once registered prostitute. This was a tempestuous relationship (Gould, 1920, Chs.3 & 4; Manuel, 1965, p.261). It suffered the financial and psychological hardships of Comte's failure to gain an academic post and the inability of this great logical thinker to manage his emotions when his wife lapsed into wayward behaviour. Comte embarked in 1826 on giving a series of lectures on Positive Philosophy in his own apartment (Gould, 1920, p.26). With the added stress of his hard work regime, he suffered a major mental breakdown from which he was not expected to recover (Manuel, 1965, p.261). He was briefly institutionalized at Charenton, then released 'not cured' to the care of his wife. He attempted suicide in 1827, but was rescued from drowning by a soldier (Gould, 1920, p.29). Nursed back to health by his wife, Comte resumed giving his course of lectures in 1829.

Following his breakdown, Comte engaged in a closed minded practice which he referred to as 'cerebral hygiene' (Mill, 1865, p.128; Hayek, 1952, p.169) in which he refused to study any works which were not in agreement with his positivist scheme. This closed mindedness led Comte to increasingly fall behind the scientific advances of his time. Living in increasing isolation, he eked a living as a mathematics entrance examiner at the Ecole Polytechnic. Meanwhile, he focussed his great powers of concentration on the development of his six volume Course of Positive Philosophy. His suppressed emotions were vented in occasional outbursts of anger against his wife. On the completion of the Positive Philosophy in 1842, Caroline left him for the last time (Gould, 1920, p.47).

Comte's extreme formality, the repression of his feelings and his lack of tact were not endearing features. Being denied a teaching post, he came to develop a persecution complex. He derided scientists as small minded specialists. His Positive Philosophy indicated that they had little to offer toward the great task of social re-building (Martineau, 1855, pp.34-36, 437-438). There were also personal quarrels and recriminations (Gould, 1920, pp.46-47; Manuel, 1965, pp.261-262; Coser, 1977, pp.18-19) leading to the loss of his examiner post. Comte was becoming increasingly reclusive and messianic, convinced that he had a mission to accomplish in his works.

A crucial biographical event in Comte's life and the turn of his works arrived in 1844. He met the young Clothilde de Vaux, a married woman whose husband had deserted her (Gould, 1920, Ch.6). They fell in love, but her tragic death in 1846 brought an outpouring of Comte's previously repressed affections (Sokoloff, 1975). He came to worship her as the personification of all that was virtuous in women (Gould, 1920, pp.74-76; Comte, 1874, Preface). In his works from this time, the most significant being the System of Positive Polity, altruistic feeling claimed ascendency over reason as the basis for social cohesion in the future positivist society – now a 'sociocracy', headed by a priestly type spiritual elite. Much of his mature life Comte had not just dedicated to developing the intellectual foundation for a new social order, but through poverty, a highly frugal lifestyle and increasingly isolated existence, provided a moral exemplar of a spiritual leader in the waiting.

For many admirers of the systematic logic of his earlier works, this change indicated the sad decline of a once great intellect (Mill, 1865, p.199. Part 2 deals with The Later Speculations of M. Comte). Mrs. Comte and Emile Littre, who had greatly admired Comte's early works, made an unsuccessful attempt, some years after Comte's death in 1857, to have his later works suppressed on the grounds of his insanity (Manuel, 1965, p.267). However, others have viewed the later works as a great contribution to Comte's system, filling out areas neglected in his earlier works with reference to the religion of humanity, his plan for the regeneration of western societies and his emphasis on aesthetics and the priority of feeling over intellect.

Comte's view of history: the perfection of moral integration

During much of the period of their alliance, Comte and Saint Simon shared a similar outlook on history. For both writers, historical change was neither directionless nor comprised of random detailed events. Instead, both adopted a high altitude view which divided history into broad sequential stages and an organicism which emphasised the importance of grasping the essential interconnectedness of social wholes prior to analysing their constituent social elements. They shared a sympathetic evaluation of feudalism and Catholicism as a period of social order and European cohesion, with Saint Simon introducing the works of the Catholic Counter-Revolutionists de Bonald and de Maistre to Comte (Maus, 1962, Ch.2). Both also provided an idealist explanation of social progress, emphasising the disruptive effect on the social organism of the decline in the world view of Catholicism and the advance of critical rationalism. And although Comte demonstrated some democratic credentials in an early essay (Separation of Opinions from Aspirations, in Fletcher, 1974), they shared an elitism which differentiated between the purely scientific knowledge used by administrative elites and the need for science to be conveyed in the form of an appropriate dogma for the masses.

From his early works, Comte was critical of conventional approaches to the study of history which viewed society as an aggregate of 'facts'. He argued that without prior recognition of an overall social framework applied within historical context, there would exist no means for the selection or interpretation of historical facts. This is because society through history is a moving entity. Even the ideas of individuals of genius are encapsulated within the culture of their times. Thus, they can at best actualise the state of play of cultural development during the times in which they live. For Comte, an overview of history revealed that cultural and intellectual progress was approaching a stage where for the first time the scientific realization of social laws was possible. Within this context, he would supply the organising genius to reveal the scientifically established direction that the course of history was taking and from which could be extrapolated the social constitution of the future.

Saint Simon had persisted with his two stage militant and industrial typology along with the alternation of critical and positive stages in his periodization of history. His works only sketched what Comte later systematized as the hierarchy of the sciences and they barely implied a law of the three stages which Comte derived from Turgot. Comte's genius was, in what he felt to be his momentous (Manuel, 1965, p.258) 1822 essay entitled Plan of the Scientific Operations Necessary for Reorganising Society (Reproduced in Fletcher, 1974) to interrelate these laws. The logical consequences for Comte of the combining of these laws will be dealt with in the following section. For the present, it is sufficient to establish that thenceforth Comte tended to disregard the militant and industrial typology and to periodized history into three main stages: a theological stage, a metaphysical stage and a positivist stage, the latter referring to the immanent future.

The earliest civilizations Comte regarded as adopting a polytheistic outlook; events on earth were seen as controlled by powerful mystical forces at the disposal of numerous gods. Over time, monotheism (belief in one god) replaced polytheism. For Comte, this enabled the theological stage to reach its zenith in feudal society of the eleventh to twelfth centuries, providing in the dogma of Catholicism heightened social order within and between nations. However, from approximately the fourteenth century, advances in philosophy were slowly eroding the Catholic world view. Increasingly, philosophical systems of thinking provided alternatives to Catholicism, culminating in a fierce rationalistic attack on clericism around the middle of the eighteenth century and bringing fully into play a metaphysical stage of philosophical criticism which spawned the French Revolution. The period of critical philosophy and social anarchy would be transcended by the application of science to all phenomena for the positivist future to emerge.

Comte argued that in the meantime, throughout the post-Revolution decades, the absence of an appropriate positive social doctrine upon which to base reconstruction had left society oscillating between republican and monarchical regimes. In Comte's view, whilst Napoleon

Bonaparte had restored order, he had subverted the course of progress through militarism and the re-establishment of Catholicism as the majority religion. The Bourbon Restoration became increasingly retrogressive. The regime ultimately aimed to turn back history by re-establishing the ancient regime and the theological outlook. And the constitutional monarchy of Louis Philippe, whilst economically progressive, provided no moral or intellectual basis for social reconstruction. It represented only the sectional interests of a narrow upper middle class elite and adopted highly repressive measures against workers. To Comte, the uniting of social cohesion and order with progress required the systematic development and propagation of a coherent social doctrine which was above sectional interests and in tune with the modernising forces of science and industry.

For Comte, the heritage of centralization, the spiritual unity of Catholicism, and progressivist rational thinking culminating in his own positivism made France amenable to positivist reconstruction. By contrast, in England, the metaphysical phase was more deeply entrenched. It exhibited itself in the liberalizing tendencies of the Reformation, parliamentary institutions and the influence of the political economists, collectively providing an environment which emphasised the importance of individual rights and freedoms at the expense of social duties. Despite her industrial advance, England's progress to the positivist era (somewhat in contrast to her more advanced role in Saint Simon's writings) was thus likely to be retarded (Comte, 1875, Vol.1, pp.66-67, 313). Comte, like the Saint Simonians, indicted the regime of Louis Philippe as a pale imitation of English constitutional monarchy which could not take root in France (Comte, 1875, Vol.1, pp.54-55).

Saint Simon had emphasised the industrial nature of the emerging society. For some time he viewed a centrally regulated industrial order and the proliferation of the cult of science as an adequate basis for a new social cohesion. Comte never viewed this as sufficient. As the Catholic Church came to adopt a reactionary stance to the Revolution of 1848, a significant proportion of working people became alienated from its influence (Moody, 1953, Pt.2, Ch.1). Fearing the growing appeal of socialism, Comte came to envisage a future 'sociocracy' built around the powerful integrating symbolism of a religion of humanity (Comte, 1875, Vol.1, pp.309-313; Bowle, 1954, pp.127-132). He supported the political dictatorship of Louis Napoleon which he believed offered a stepping stone toward a positivist republic. Centralized temporal rule to maintain social order during a period of 'spiritual interregnum' (Comte, 1875, Vol.1, pp.304-309) would allow time for the propagation of positivism to fill the spiritual void and eventually reduce the need for political repression. His utopia of a highly stable positivist French republic was, he thought, about a generation away.

The intellectual establishment of positivism I
'Positivism' had different connotations at different stages of Comte's work (Charlton, 1959, Ch.1-3). In this section, the intellectual foundations of positivism which Comte believed he had set out in his 1822 essay Plan for the Scientific Operations Necessary for Reorganizing Society and developed in the Positive Philosophy will be reviewed.

Comte felt that post-Revolution France remained in a condition of loss; loss of social stability and moral integration. Despite the imposition of political order, society lurched from one regime to another. He believed that this was an abnormal social condition which had been ultimately brought about by Enlightenment doctrines that were critical of the old order. These doctrines emphasised individual rights as opposed to social duties and precipitated the Revolution. This condition required termination.

Comte adopted a thoroughgoing idealist analysis of history. It pointed to the inevitable emergence of a stable and durable social order. Certainty of this depended on the demonstration of laws of intellectual progress. These Comte believed he had discovered in the combination of his law of the three stages and the hierarchy of the sciences.

The law of the three stages was first put forward by Comte in his landmark 1822 essay as an orientating hypothesis which, he acknowledged, was open to modification and refinement by future research. However, this law become more systematically entrenched into his system in the Positive Philosophy. According to this law (Martineau, 1855, Book 1, Ch.1), prior to becoming scientific, all areas of knowledge began at a theological stage and passed through a metaphysical stage. At the theological stage, the phenomena in question were explained as created and determined by the volitions of divinities. Polytheistic belief systems tended to be superseded by monotheistic religions. Divinities were viewed subjectively, inspiring feelings and passions of love, fear and awe. By the metaphysical stage, theological interpretations gave way to the philosophical outlook that mysterious forces in the form of entities inherent within phenomena determined its behaviour. When applied to social phenomena, these flights of imagination provided unsubstantiated and unworkable philosophical schemes in which the direction of change and final outcome remained uncertain (Bury, 1920, p,305). Claiming to be rational, but without grounding in the scientific study of phenomena, in practice these schemes could only lead to social disasters. However, having dissolved theological thinking, their role was to provide a stepping stone toward the final positivist stage of thinking in which the concrete laws of phenomena become revealed through the process of rigorous observation, comparison, experimentation and historical method, enabling expert intervention to regulate the social condition for the general well-being.

The cornerstone of Comte's positivism was the assertion that all phenomena operate according to laws. His hierarchy of the sciences (Martineau, 1855, Book 1, Ch.2) indicated a sequential spread of scientific knowledge. It referred to both the logical and historical order in which the laws at work in different levels of phenomena were uncovered in the progress of knowledge – a law explaining man's discovery of laws. The logical sequence was based on the complexity and generality of the subject matter. Human understanding could only first apply scientific reasoning to the least complex and most general phenomena. Mathematics was therefore the first discipline to make the journey to science through religion and metaphysics. Similarly, through theological and metaphysical stages, scientific knowledge then had to make a sequential ascent through astronomy, physics, chemistry, biology and finally to the most complex and least general of phenomena in sociology. For example, once the study of the planets broke free from the theological viewpoint, a metaphysical outlook emerged in the form of astrology before it became the positive science of astronomy which applied mathematics, scientific concepts and observation to uncover the laws of planetary motion. Likewise, and subsequently, the science of chemistry was reached through the metaphysics of alchemy. The study of society, being the most complex and the last to make this journey, being still embroiled in the metaphysical stage, would soon ascend to becoming a positive science. Because of the complexity of the realm to which it applies, sociological knowledge could never hope to be complete, but would be adequate for the purpose of social reconstruction.

Chart summarising Comte's law of the three stages and hierarchy of the sciences (Pullinger, 2014, p36)

Hierarchy of sciences

Sociology	T			M	P
Biology	T		M		P
Chemistry ⵗ	T		M	P	
Physics	T	M		P	
Astronomy	T	M		P	
Mathematics	P				

| 1200s | 1400s | 1600s | 1800s |

Time and law of three stages →

Key: T = Theological

M = Metaphysical

P = Positivist

The development of the lower order sciences offered insights for science to gain a foothold into their immediate successors on the hierarchy. For Comte, given the complexity of social phenomena, scientific understanding of the social organism required the assistance of an established biological science. Scientific method and understanding having worked its way up to biology, sociology, the science of society, remained the final and imminent area of scientific conquest. It could gain from the insights of and by analogy from biological science that organisms had laws of statics (functional integration) and dynamics (maturational change).

Comte maintained that the hierarchy of the sciences indicated that the laws of different levels of phenomena operated within differing margins of variability. Lower level inorganic phenomena were strictly determined. The laws of astronomy and physics could therefore be reducible to mathematical formulae. Those applicable to society, the highest and most complex level of phenomena, exhibited the greatest margin of variability. They were consequently the least reducible to representation in the form of mathematical formulae (Martineau, 1855, Book 1, pp.367-38) and offered the greatest scope for human intervention. This, Comte referred to as 'modifiable fatality' (Comte, 1875, Vol.1, pp.42-43).

Comte's sociological holism rested on a fundamental distinction between the scientific approach appropriate to the inorganic and the organic sciences. Scientific knowledge of the laws of inorganic phenomena derived from an analysis of elements, often with the aid of mathematics. An analytic and atomistic approach by which the whole could be explained through a study of the elements was appropriate. However, in the study of organic phenomena, elements could only be understood synthetically, through prior apprehension of the whole as an entity. Knowledge of the elements of society (the smallest of which he regarded to be not individuals but the family), the highest organic phenomena, therefore required prior understanding of the interconnectedness of the social whole.

The hierarchy of the sciences also expressed levels of interdependence in phenomena. Knowledge of lower level sciences was not only a necessary guide to the procedures of the sciences above them, but the laws by which a level of phenomena behaved were dependent on those of lower level phenomena, without being entirely determined by them. Soundly based laws of social phenomena must therefore await our knowledge of biological laws. They would otherwise be premature. Should premature attempts to establish social laws subsequently be found to contradict what biological laws come to tell us about the human condition, they must be incorrect and discounted as guides to behaviour.

For Comte, when combining the law of the three stages with the hierarchy of the sciences and applying his idealist position, the stage reached by the prevailing social doctrine determined the social condition. Organically integrated doctrines (theological and positivist) provided systems of thinking which bound individuals to the social organism. Negative doctrines (metaphysical) were ego promoting and led to social instability and anarchy. It would require understanding of society to reach the scientific stage to adopt a holistic vantage point and establish a new social cohesion on the foundation of knowledge of social laws. Comte argued that this will lead to the highest form of social order, since the transition from theological, through metaphysical to scientific will have spread right up the hierarchy of the sciences to embrace an understanding of the laws of all phenomena, thus providing the ultimate intellectual consensus.

Like Saint Simon, Comte distinguished between the spiritual and the temporal hierarchy. The spiritual sphere referred to moral integration based on a prevailing social dogma. The temporal sphere was that of power politics. Under Catholicism, at the height of its influence, he claimed that the spiritual sphere was ascendant over temporal matters. It overrode temporal disharmony. In undermining the old spiritual harmony and authority, critical philosophy unleashed social instability. Under these circumstances, temporal power had to impose its rule where a socially constructive spiritual influence was absent. For Comte, this accounted for Napoleon Bonaparte's post–Revolution dictatorship in which the Catholic religion was only reinstated as part of a blueprint to support the political regime. Without spiritual ascendency, temporal power remained inherently unstable. Social stability could only be re-established when an organic social dogma appropriate to the new age was sufficiently developed and taken up by the masses. Comte argued that his laws of intellectual progress showed that positivism must perform this role, enabling temporal dictatorship to recede. Whether political dictatorship would necessarily recede, of course, is another question (Acton, 1951).

The Enlightenment philosophes viewed society as comprised of individual units, each with rights. This promoted egoism which Comte maintained, at the expense of duty, undermined the social fabric. It also encouraged a preoccupation with psychology, a subject which Comte believed was purely speculative in regarding internal subjective states which could not be directly observed. These states were in fact the outcome of objective external influences which could be observed. Psychology, therefore, had no place in his hierarchy of the sciences. Furthermore, Comte criticised Enlightenment views of social 'science' that anticipated basing a 'science' of society on the analytic approach of applying mathematics to an aggregate study of individuals as reductionist (to the procedures of the lower sciences) and criticised Condorcet for anticipating such an empirical approach to social science. Reductionism was also a charge that could be made against those who searched for a sole concept to explain the behaviour of all levels of phenomena, a criticism which could be applied to Saint Simon's speculation on the concept of gravity, and, as we shall later see, to Spencer's evolutionism.

Comte opposed the fragmentation of science and belittled the activities of specialists as trivial. Moreover, for him the fragmentation of the study of society into specialist areas such as politics and economics was counterproductive. In England, the appeal of the apparent science of political economy reflected the traits of liberalism and the hallmark of metaphysical thinking. It regarded the natural basis of industrial society to be a harmony of individual utilitarian interests. For Comte, whilst the political economists claimed to have discovered the laws through which free market forces operated, they had to fall back on the pre-scientific and metaphysical notion of the 'invisible hand' guiding the process. And just as any analysis of society deriving an understanding of the whole from an aggregate of its parts would be ill conceived, so a 'society' itself in which individual needs prevailed over social needs would be a social monstrosity. It would either disintegrate into anarchy or could hold together only through extreme coercion. In response, John Stuart Mill (1865), although impressed by Comte's early works, argued that he had defined the characteristics of the metaphysical stage too broadly. In generalising his theory from the French context, Mill claimed, Comte did not appreciate the extent to which England could be Protestant, liberal and orderly.

However, for Comte, critical ideas of individual rights and equality had served their progressive purpose in the destruction of theological ideas and feudal institutions. They were not a fit basis for social reconstruction. As Comte put it 'weapons of war cannot be metamorphosed into instruments of construction' (Comte, reproduced in Fletcher, 1974, p.117). The political 'freedoms' and rights of parliamentary democracy, were no basis for moral integration or sound intervention. Only the development of positivist social science would be able to indicate the range of intelligent social interventionism to assist the progress and harmony of the social organism. It would be the science of the possible which would be needed to restrain the unrealistic ambitions of political leaders and dampen down insatiable expectations opened up by the Revolution. The liberty of positivism would be constructive. Positivist freedom would equate to freedom from the destructive consequences of acting in ignorance of social laws.

Positivism II: social progress toward sociocracy

Comte completed his last major work, System of Positive Polity, between 1851 and 1854. In this work he argued that he had now surpassed the arid intellectualism of the Positive Philosophy (Comte, 1875, Vol.1, Preface & Ch.1). He still claimed the validity of his the law of the three stages and the hierarchy of the sciences, to which he added the now highest science of morals. Indeed, he evaluated the stages of his own works with reference to these laws (Comte, 1875, Vol.1, Ch.2). His earlier works were viewed as a product of the late metaphysical stage, a period during which the intellect was seen as supreme. The Revolution of 1789 had represented the destructive height of the metaphysical stage. Comte now argued that his 1822 essay, in which he had first demonstrated his two key laws of progress, signalled the beginning of the second phase of the metaphysical stage. This was a more constructive phase in which he was able to appeal to science and the intellect to demonstrate the logical and historical imminence of the positivist order. Now, following the Revolution of 1848 and the rise to power of Louis Napoleon, he believed its arrival to be close at hand. Comte became preoccupied with delineating its altruistic and religious nature in the form of a new spiritual order for the purpose of propagating its emergence.

Comte had emphasised in his Positive Philosophy that man would outgrow theological explanations of social phenomena. Instead, a this-worldly view of social phenomena would be the basis for a new social order. In the Positive Polity, Comte now argued that in the positivist society the this-worldly view would comprise the highest religious and moral state. Theological thinking, dominated by belief in supernatural forces, would become surpassed by the 'religion of humanity'. Artists would play a key role in idealising humanity through devising festivals and ceremonies devoted to the achievements of the greatest contributors to humanity (identified with reference to Comte's laws of progress), thus enhancing the altruistic bond as a basis for social cohesion. Comte now placed at the pinnacle of his society not a positivist technocratic elite, but a priest like elite, vested in their calming authority as moral arbiters in temporal disputes. The image of a positivist society was now being replaced by that of a 'sociocracy'. What accounted for this new twist in Comte's positivism and what were its implications?

The answer to the first question can be brief and is mainly found at the biographical level. Following his breakdown, Comte practiced what he called 'cerebral hygiene'. Whilst anticipating the final conquest of science, Comte had adopted the highly unscientific stance of intolerance to ideas at odds with his positivism. Snubbed by academia, he increasingly isolated himself in the world of his own works.

In 1844, Comte met the sensitive, intelligent but soon ailing Catholic woman Clotilde de Vaux. He was in love for the first time in his life. When she died in 1846, Comte was devastated. Overcome by an outpouring of feelings, Comte worshipped her daily as a saint (Comte, 1874, Preface & pp.13-16; Manuel, 1965, p,265; Sokoloff, 1975, Ch.9), symbolising the altruistic qualities of women. His mania for religion and ritual which surfaces in his works post-dates this time.

Comte was now aiming at a new audience for his positivism. The overthrow of the regime that he detested, the Bourgeois Monarchy, in 1848 and the emergence of the Second Republic under the dictatorship of Louis Napoleon offered, he felt, a stepping stone to a sociocratic republic (Comte 1875, Vol.1, pp.55-58 & pp.306-309). In his propagandist work for the new order, The Catechism of Positive Religion, completed during the writing of Positive Polity, Comte referred in July 1852 to 'the fortunate crisis which has just abolished the Parliamentary regime and instituted a dictatorial republic' (Comte, 1874, Preface, p.8). The urgent requirement was now to assist the transition to the anticipated sociocracy.

The intellectual middle classes had ignored his earlier works. His scheme had always been critical of middle class academics whose intellectual specializations, he argued, could contribute little toward promoting the cohesive overview that was much needed for the establishment of the new social order. In his Positive Polity, he now attacked their egoism and intellectualism as divisive and praised what he regarded as the superior qualities of altruism of the working classes and women. The new social order would require their adherence under the wise guidance of a positivist 'priesthood' who would be autonomous from the temporal hierarchy and intervene in society independently of sectional interests.

In appealing to the working classes, Comte was aware of the allure of communism. He argued that communism mistakenly intended to overthrow both the spiritual and temporal hierarchy. For Comte, in the interests of social continuity, private property must be maintained. Acquiring political power by the masses should not be the aim of social regeneration, but instead its moral regulation for the common good under the wise guidance of a spiritual elite (Comte, 1875, Vol.1, Ch.3), ultimately to be headed by himself.

With reference to 'the unfortunate exercise of universal suffrage' (Comte, 1874, p.18), Comte advocated that the masses, in whom in particular the sympathies governed the intellect, should accept their lack of influence within the temporal sphere of power. Through their altruism, they would be morally superior to the egoistic middle classes. In the sociocracy, workers would be liberated from the anarchy of a society that had prioritised individual rights over social duty. They would find compensation for the hardships consequent on their lowly place in the temporal hierarchy by their liberation from the responsibilities that weighed over leaders and decision makers and comforted by the solace of the religion of humanity.

To Comte, a 'spiritual interregnum' existed which had to be bridged for the sociocratic republic to be reached. To do so would require a generation of political dictatorship to provide a breathing space in which the population would be appropriately re-educated and re-socialised. For this purpose, Comte advocated the need to establish a common education following his hierarchy of the sciences, an arrangement which tallied with his view that the maturation process of the individual mind recapitulates the stages of intellectual progress followed by society and humanity. This new ordering of education would supersede what he viewed as the unsystematic education of the middle classes that was so characteristic of the metaphysical phase. Positivist education would be supplemented by the guidance of popular discussion and public opinion by the positivist 'priesthood'. Social cohesion would be enhanced as the temporal order became tamed by the emergent new moral altruism and spiritual order.

Comte's religion of humanity would contemplate the past, present and future of mankind, the 'supreme being', as the object of worship. By commemorating mankind's greatest contributors, in contrast to theology prayer would not be for the self-interested motive of protection by a mystical divine power but the altruistic motive of reconciliation to humanity through thanksgiving (Comte, 1874, Comte, 1875, Vol.1, Ch.6). The temporal hierarchy of individual competition and political power would become increasingly under the sway of the growing influence of the spiritual hierarchy of moral worth. Artists may envisage the future as a society engulfed by this spiritual order as a worthy utopian image grounded in the laws of progress.

The great English liberal theorist J.S.Mill found much to admire in the synthesising logic of Comte's early works (Mill, 1865, Part 1). He became shocked, as had Littre, by the mania for systematization, the dogma, and the ritual which he found in the later works (Mill, 1865, Part II). For Mill, these works represented the degeneration of a once great intellect.

T.H.Huxley found in Comte's later works 'Catholicism minus Christianity' (Hayek, 1952, p.184; Bowle, 1954, p.130). Similarly, one may refer to Comte's religion of humanity as a type of de-theologised Catholicism and the notion of the 'supreme being' of humanity as the object of worship as a metaphysical abstraction.

Comte's social laws and the question of freedom

There is, then, clear evidence of growing dogma and authoritarianism in Comte's later works. This can be illustrated by considering the nature and purpose of social laws in his scheme. In outlining his hierarchy of the sciences, Comte originally emphasised that the lower level phenomena operated closely to the constraints of mathematical laws, whilst the highest level of phenomena, the social, proceed within laws of a far broader scope, ultimately allowing for intelligent human intervention when they become known. Whether man was blind to these laws or not, they must still operate. Acting blindly to social laws simply implied greater social disturbance as ill-informed social and political decisions were made. Conversely, knowledge of social laws enabled social turbulence to be minimized as social technicians steered society well within the bounds of the laws, easing the path of progress. This interpretation finds support in the following quotation:

> 'There is a great difference between obeying the progress of civilization blindly and obeying it intelligently. The changes it

demands take place as much in the first as in the second case; but they are longer delayed, and, above all, are only accomplished after having produced social perturbations more or less serious, according to the nature and importance of these changes. Now the disturbances of every sort, which thus arise in the body politic, may be, in great part, avoided by adopting measures based on an exact knowledge of the changes which tend to produce themselves' (Comte, 1875, Vol.4, p.560).

In summary, Comte was saying that our ignorance of social laws places society at the mercy of greater disruptions. Liberty from the latter can only arrive with knowledge of and rational submission to social laws (Hayek, 1952, Ch.6).

However, another interpretation of social laws would cause greater problems for Comte. Again, taking his hierarchy of the sciences as the point of departure, it could be argued that our ignorance of social laws would render us blindly subordinate to them. We would be governed by laws closer to the type operating in the non-thinking physical world. By contrast, knowledge of social laws may incline decision makers toward social intervention against the undesired consequences that they point to and toward desired outcomes. Blind fatality would then give way to modifiable fatality and the very possibility of social laws would seem to conflict with liberation from them that intervention based on the prevision that knowing them gives. According to this interpretation, social laws could only operate in our ignorance of them. Knowing them would liberate us from their strict necessity. But this is the last thing that Comte desires. In his propagandist work, the emphasis moves away from the need for scientific exactitude in social laws and reveals his true unscientific desires.

'the ignorance of these laws is, for our action, equivalent to their non-existence, as it precludes all rational prevision, and so all regular interference. Still we may hope to discover for each of the more important cases, empirical rules which, insufficient from the theoretic point of view, yet suffice to keep us from disorderly action' (Comte, 1874, p.114).

In this work, Comte, who cast himself in the role of the priest, conducted an imaginary dialogue with the woman he had loved but whose death had robbed him of time to convert her to his positivism. He used the process of conversion to appeal in religious overtones to the altruism of women and the masses to submit to social laws.

Priest: 'When the higher laws shall be sufficiently known, the Positive priesthood will draw from them results more precious and susceptible of greater regularity than those of the most perfect astronomy. For the previsions of astronomy become uncertain, and often unattainable, as soon as the planetary problems become very complicated........the providence of man can, and ought to aspire to give more regularity to the order which is most amenable to its action, than can prevail, as regards the majority of events, in the order which obeys only a blind fatality. The greater complication of the phenomena will ultimately yield, in these high cases, to the paramount sagacity of the modifying agent, when the human order shall be sufficiently known.'

Woman: 'I feel, my father, that to subordinate the subjective to the objective is at once the constant obligation and the chief resource of Positive worship' (Comte, 1874, pp.71-72).

Now, it would appear that through intervention, order in society can reach a higher level of perfection than is the case with planetary motion. Subjectivity for Comte referred to the individual mind. Objectivity referred to social laws. Comte was now appealing to social laws the more to emphasise individual subordination to them. His earlier emphasis through the hierarchy of the sciences on the greater complication and limited exactitude of social knowledge was now overridden by the criteria of greater possibility of intervention. Social laws may be less certain than physical laws, but behaviour may be regulated into closer conformity to them. Now, his 'positivism' had become a social dogma which insisted that laws that apparently already operate in the social realm must be rigidly imposed by man! Social interventionism which he once related to the modifiable fatality of social phenomena became an imposed fatality as absolute as divine providence.

Comte's law of the three stages initially posited a fixed sequence of social and intellectual progress. The metaphysical stage had to intervene in between theological and positivistic societies because theology and science were modes of thinking too antagonistic for a smooth transition to take place. However, he later came to emphasise that his law of progress did not require each society to laboriously reproduce the stages of history of the more advanced nations (Manuel, 1965, p.280). This may have been a valid modification to his scheme which distinguished between modernization taking place ignorant of social laws and that which was later guided by knowledge of social laws and the example of early modernizers. However, it is also evident that Comte's outlook had become increasingly anti-Enlightenment and more Medievalist. The positivist society came to resemble the ordered society of the feudalism. In Comte's mania for regulation, social anarchy was to be avoided at all costs. With the painful example of French modernization and the emergence of his theory for guidance, the religious stages of theocracy and positivist sociocracy would become capable of squeezing out the despised metaphysical stage in some subsequent modernizations. Thus, Comte argued that Italy and Spain, though regarded as economically backward, could be navigated quickly from Catholicism to the positivist sociocracy, largely jumping the metaphysical stage (Comte, 1875, Vol.1, pp.216-217).

A similar view was adopted toward Islam. In a letter to Reschid Pacha, ruler of Turkey, Comte referred to the possibility of 'passing straight from Islamism to Positivism, without any metaphysical transition' (Comte, 1875, Vol.3, Preface, p.XLIII).

'The final regeneration may triumph in the East without arousing the anarchical agitation to which the West was condemned by its initiative' (Comte, 1875, Vol.3, Preface, p.XLIII).

In political terms, Comte's aversion for social disorder translated into the preference for a progressive dictatorship steering the modernization process from above toward a sociocratic republic. Writing to Tzar Nicholas I of Russia, Comte advised that:

'When the meritorious chiefs of Eastern Europe know by observation of the Western case the necessary goal – in their own case more distant – of the universal movement, they can thenseforward smooth the way for, and at the same time hasten its attainment in their own countries, by preserving their peoples from the storms that marked the first renovation. Cautiously moving in advance of their respective civilizations, their business is to direct the final transition from theocracy into sociocracy' (Comte, 1875, Vol.3, Preface, p.XXXVIII).

Comte's early positivism had retained the scientific emphasis of the Enlightenment. His republicanism was supported by his social laws. His social laws then came to indicate that although society could not return to the theology of the ancien regime, a new social cohesion required a secular religion. The notion of 'humanity' associated with the French Revolution had been a liberating one – an attack on the privileges of the old regime. Comte's religion of humanity retained its secular orientation but closed down the liberating dimension. Ritualism and symbolism were recognized as just as important to the moral order of a republican sociocracy as they had been under Catholicism and the old order. Here, as Nisbet (1970, Chs.1 & 2) claims, was certainly a conservative reaction in the founding of French sociology to the social dislocations of the French Revolution. Initially proposed as an orientating hypothesis, Comte's law of the three stages became intellectually systematised, dogmatically asserted and finally the foundation for an authoritarian sociocracy. In the process, authoritarian impatience came to take over from intellectual integrity.

Prophets of Progress: Saint Simon, Comte and Spencer

4 | A Sketch of the English Historical Background to the Theory of Spencer

Different sections of society may be identified by their community of ideas and image of the current society, by their place in it and an awareness of a beneficial direction of social change from their perspective. These images and ideals need to be represented in a system of thinking that claims both intellectual integrity and emotional resonance. In the struggle between the social ideals of different social classes, Harold Perkin has maintained that what was required was:

'a conscious image of the class in its relation to rival classes, and of the ideal society in which it would find its rightful place. The troops, or at least a considerable portion of them, had to have some notion of the army as a whole and its position relative to the enemy, and of the objective at which they were aiming. Moreover, since morale was half the battle, the image had to be flattering to one's own side and demoralizing to one's opponents; it had to be an ideal image of the representative member of one's own class as the lynchpin of society, the only role-bearer who fully justified his place, the ideal citizen whom the rest should emulate, and of the ideal society as one in which this ideal citizen would be suitably honoured and rewarded' (Perkin, 1972, p.219).

Herbert Spencer's social theory was such a weapon in the armoury of entrepreneurial ideas. It located the entrepreneurialism of the industrial middle class of early capitalism at the heart of the modernization process and reflected his own lower middle class social background of voluntarist education, religious dissent and free enterprise values. His social theory justified these features as virtues of English modernization and built them into his powerful broader theory of universal evolution. Quite different criteria of modernization had been central to the social theories of Saint Simon and Comte in the battle between ideals which they waged in the context of French modernization.

This chapter will form a macro and historical context on English modernization as the broader setting for Spencer's social theory. It establishes a tradition of science, sobriety, and industriousness which runs from seventeenth century Puritanism through religious dissent to nineteenth century utilitarianism and laissez faire. This tradition was Spencer's intellectual heritage, a tradition which opposed the privilege and indulgence of the landed aristocracy and the relative splendour and ceremonial show of the established church.

In England, the demise of feudalism set in relatively early. Commercial influences, argues Barrington Moore, were effectively penetrating agriculture from the Middle Ages (1967, pp.3-14). Landowners were using their land for profit rather than, as in France, for the extension of time honoured obligations from the peasantry (Barrington Moore, 1967, p.8). This was a prelude to agricultural efficiency and the transition of the peasantry to the status of agricultural labourers which was later enhanced by the enclosure of common land for agricultural use, a process which was under way during the sixteenth century (Barrington Moore, 1967, pp.9-14).

Royal absolutism – the centralization of power under the monarchy and the unification of society which accompanied the decay of feudal localism (Anderson, 1984, Ch.1) – was relatively short lived in England. Anderson dates this phase to have run from the early 1500s to 1640. Furthermore, it did not reach the same intensity as in France (Anderson, 1984, Ch.5) where it provided a framework for the advance of commerce but within an antiquated structure of feudal privileges which limited commercial freedom and growth (Anderson, 1984, Ch.4). In England, in contrast to France, engagement in commercial activities by the landed orders was not accompanied by the risk of derogation of social status.

The break with the Church of Rome in the sixteenth century had advanced the Reformation in England. Without the sanction of the Catholic religion, royal absolutism and the divine right of kings could not be so powerfully established. The 'revolutionary' changes of the seventeenth century – the victory of the Parliamentarians in the Civil War during the middle decades and the 'Revolution' of 1688 (although whether the latter merits the term Revolution which Whig historians had attributed to it is highly questionable (Watson, 1973)) – brought the end of royal absolutism, signified the influence of Puritanism, and finally established the Protestant religion and a constitutional monarchy.

Under the Protestant constitution, Protestant sects were tolerated, compared to their persecution in Catholic France. Such a contrast has been related to the relative prospects for economic modernization. Weber (1978) has argued that Catholicism was less conducive to the tension and dynamism associated with economic modernization than those ascetic Protestant sects which placed the onus of proof of salvation worthiness on the this-worldly success of the individual, without offering the emotional release of the confessional for those who strayed from the path of righteousness. This, Weber argued, encouraged in the believer a restless industriousness and austerity which were conducive to but did not alone cause the emergence of modern rational capitalism.

In similar vein, a link has been drawn by Merton (1970) between Puritanism and scientific advance in England. Merton argued that the literal mindedness embodied in Puritanism had an affinity with the practical and empirical character of science. By the mid-seventeenth century, the physical science had acquired an improved occupational status and a disproportionately high adherence of Puritans – later even within the Royal Society.

Following the 'Revolution' of 1688, the establishment of a constitutional monarchy enhanced the power of a Parliament of commercially minded landowners vis-à-vis that of the crown. For Whig historians, the constitutional monarchy represented the 'perfect constitution' – a political system responsive to pressures for necessary reforms which provided a guarantee of smooth change. In fact, whilst the constitution gave the landlords in Parliament a safeguard against excessive crown interference, they did not intend to devolve power down the social order more than was necessary, but were happy to manipulate a tiny electorate. As late as 1830, only about 1% of the population were entitled to vote. And whilst the constitution guaranteed religious tolerance, it did not provide equal social rights for dissenters.

Nevertheless, by the late seventeenth century England was a relatively open and liberal society compared to France where the remnants of feudalism remained. In France, high office could be purchased, owned and inherited. Peasants were taxed severely whilst the nobility were largely exempt. Commerce and industry were tightly regulated and internal customs barriers were commonplace. Religious persecution drove industrious dissenters to emigrate and many, such as communities of Huguenots, arrived in England (Williams, 1970, p.188 & p.520). French Enlightenment writers such as Voltaire admired the relative religious and commercial freedoms of England.

England by the eighteenth century did not comprise a social hierarchy of rigid estates. The aristocracy were not exempt from taxation nor governed by vastly different laws than commoners. Freedom of internal trade and absolute property rights had been established. Land transactions associated with the commercialization of agriculture were relatively frequent, reducing the preoccupation with tracing noble lineage (Williams, 1970, pp.509-512). Perkin (1972, Ch.2) has characterised this society as a relatively open social structure based on property and patronage. A wide dispersal of property made for a stable social hierarchy of many grades with significant levels of social mobility (Perkin, 1972, pp.56-62). On the eve of the Industrial Revolution, Scottish Enlightenment writers, compared to their French counterparts, were optimistic of steady progress in comfort and refined social feelings developing with advancing commercial prosperity and private property (Chitnis, 1976, Ch.5).

Being the first country to industrialize, England defied the later rule of imitative industrialization enhanced through the mechanism of the state. Relatively simple inventions by practical minded individuals required little capital but could significantly increase productivity. English industrialization was unique in its spontaneity and its development was arguably assisted by the social, economic and religious freedoms of the old society. Of particular significance for scientific and economic advance late in the old order was the position of dissenters; members of various denominations who held in common a rejection of imposed human authority and a defence of individual conscience in matters of religion. Religious dissent defined in this broad way was more a characteristic of the commercial middle ranks of the old society (Lincoln, 1971, Ch.2). Upholding as a natural right the freedom of individual conscience and freedom of enquiry, dissenters were highly represented amongst those who channelled their free thinking into scientific and philosophical matters. They were opposed to the imposition of established Church doctrine and the alliance of the Anglican Church and the state. This alliance was seen to reflect the traditional interests of the landed elite who could often influence the religious outlook of the lower social orders.

Throughout eighteenth century England, access to positions within the establishment was denied to dissenters, although with the opportunity of upward social mobility through patronage, some ambitious dissenters found it expedient to convert to Anglicanism on the way up (Perkin, 1972, pp.34-38). Entrance to Scottish universities was a possible option for dissenters, but they could not enter the traditional English universities without declaring their allegiance to the Anglican Church by subscribing to the Thirty Nine Articles. This closed off passage for many into the traditional professions. Crown offices were also closed to them through the Test and Corporation Acts. This balance of religious tolerance but imposed marginality, combined with the work ethic and spirit of free enquiry of ascetic Protestant denominations, arguably provided a social recipe to encourage dissenters to channel their energies into commerce, industry and science. They established their own schools and academies with a practical orientation in commercial subjects, science and philosophy (Lincoln, 1971, Ch.3) which were renowned for setting high educational standards. During the latter decades of the eighteenth century, scientific and philosophical societies were formed, especially in the provincial towns where religious dissent flourished (Schofield, 1963,

Ch.1). Typically interested in a broad range of sciences, experimentation and speculation and the development and improvement of mechanical devices (Schofield, 1963, Ch.2), these bodies linked science with industrial inventions and were argued to be of vital assistance in enhancing the Industrial Revolution (Robinson, 1953). Dissenters within the old order can thus be seen as the embryo of the entrepreneurial middle class of the new industrial society that their beliefs and activities encouraged the very prospects of, and dissent provided a stepping stone to middle class consciousness once the new class system had crystallized (Perkin, 1972, Ch.2 & pp.347-364).

Events of the 1770s – 1780s raised the optimism of dissenters that divine providence was on their side through advancing religious tolerance (Lincoln, 1971, Ch.6). The American War of Independence and the French Revolution initially appeared to herald the opening up of a more tolerant age. Dissenters often identified politically with advanced Whigs, forming political and correspondence societies, arguing for Parliamentary reform, and demanding religious freedom and full citizenship as natural rights (Lincoln, 1971, pp.235-256). Amongst more disadvantaged sections of society, radical literature emphasised that reason and education could overcome the obstacles of tradition (Brown, 1918, pp.43-50). Radical political societies and literature momentarily thrived (Brown, 1918, Ch.3; Gregg, 1984, pp.81-83) along with a climate of utopian optimism.

However, the reaction of traditionalists to the French Revolution found its classic statement in Burke's Reflections on the Revolution in France (1790). Burke emphasised the comfort of tradition and gradual change as natural growth as opposed to the imposition of abrasive new institutions fashioned by reason. And as the French Revolution moved to more extreme measures by 1793, the mood of opinion in England was changing. Reformist Whig aristocrats noted what had happened to French landed interests and came to distance themselves from radicals (Brown, 1918, pp.175-177). Once war was engaged in against the Republic, the government viewed all radicals, dissenters and reform societies as highly dangerous (Brown, 1918, Ch.4; Lincoln, 1971, pp.256-270) and took various repressive measures against them including the censorship of radical material (Brown, 1918, pp.83-162; Gregg, 1984, pp.78-85). A reaction in popular opinion was encouraged by the government and the established Church. Even though there appeared to be little evidence of preparation for the use of physical force (Brown, 1918, Ch.7), an atmosphere of heightened patriotism made even appeals for modest peaceful reform appear subversive and treasonable. Radicals and dissenters who saw themselves in the tradition of 1688 came to be seen by Church and King opponents as men of 1649 (Lincoln, 1971, pp.8-

9) and many suffered at the hands of mobs (Brown, 1918, pp.77-90). Consequently, dissenting and reformist opinion were driven underground by a climate of wartime patriotism, but not before it had begun to effect its economic mission.

In the context of this reaction to the French Revolution, radical Whigs who held republican sympathies had tarnished their party's image. Tory governments obstinate to social reform remained in power for most of the four decades prior to 1830. When post war depression had brought growing demonstrations, the spectre of revolution in the minds of the authorities ushered in a period of severe repressions (Gregg, 1984, pp.87-97; Rayner, 1962, Ch.5). Only from the mid-1820s were the repressions lifted as the paranoia of the authorities abated. This allowed to become manifest what had remained latent – the emergence of a new social order with opposing social classes largely replacing the finely graded hierarchy of patronage, paternalism and deference of the old order (Perkin, 1972, Ch.6).

Relations between the classes were complex and shifting. With their growing involvement in business and commerce, landowners often took a less paternalistic outlook toward the lower social orders (Perkin, 1972, pp.183-195). The Enclosure Movement had cut many workers adrift from rural and agricultural existence. For workers, often not hostile to the old order but resentful of the abdication of a degree of paternalism once offered by the landed orders (Perkin, 1972, pp.124-133), this often meant the necessity of moving from a rural to an urban setting, adjustment to more impersonal relationships associated with working within factory conditions and the insecurity of exposure to free market forces.

Especially from the ranks of the dissenting middle classes had come the inventiveness, application and enterprise behind industrialization. They were the advocates and main beneficiaries of non-interventionist reform. Prepared to support the humanitarian crusades of Evangelical reformers against slave labour abroad, they were less humanitarian regarding child labour at home (Cowherd, 1959, Ch.2), examples of which abounded in Engels' study The Conditions of the Working Class in England (1974, pp.178-181 & 216-234).

Interventionist factory legislation found support from Evangelicals and some Tories and Anglican bishops (Cowherd, 1959, Ch.2; Perkin, 1972, Ch.7); representatives of landed interests who were still prepared to demonstrate their paternalistic credentials as rightful protectors of workers from the worst ravages of industrialization, so long as the legislation was aimed at constraining an uppity urban entrepreneurial class of factory employers rather than benefiting agricultural workers. Clearly, in the struggle between ideals representing the self-interest of different social classes, there remained some life left in the paternalistic outlook of the old higher social orders to the challenge of the entrepreneurial middle classes well into the period of industrialization.

For their part, the middle classes aimed their attack on traditionalism and paternalism through the social theories of laissez faire and utilitarianism, both rooted in the ideas of political economy. Workers may have disagreed with these philosophies, but they were prepared temporarily to join forces with the middle classes in the pursuit of Parliamentary reform. In effect, the predominantly landowning Whig elite in Parliament introduced limited reform to head off a possible alliance of middle class and working class radicalism. The 1832 Reform Bill extended Parliamentary representation to the industrial towns and thus transferred some political power from the landed aristocracy to the moneyed middle classes. But the message was one of so far and no further. Aggrieved at the limited extension of the franchise to property owners, many workers saw middle class complicity in the reform which they referred to as the 'great betrayal' (Gregg, 1884, p.158).

Against the background of antagonism toward the establishment, middle class consciousness differentiated further from working class consciousness following the Reform Act (Briggs, 1956). Working class consciousness became channelled into Chartism, with the key aim of achieving universal male suffrage, and middle class consciousness became directed into a variety of single but related protest issues, the greatest movement being the Anti-Corn Law League. For the purposes of this text, attention will be focussed on the middle class movements.

Middle class radicalism reached its height in the provincial north and the midlands during the 1830s – 1840s. The Corn Laws had been firmed up at the end of the Napoleonic Wars to protect the home production of wheat and the profits of farmers by prohibiting imports until the price of wheat reached a certain level. These Laws were seen as a form of interventionist legislation, continuing in place well beyond the period of justification in the conflict with France to the benefit of the sectional interests of Anglican London landlords who still dominated Parliament. They became the target of extra-Parliamentary action by free traders – notably the provincial industrial middle classes with a strong representation of religious dissenters.

Following periodic agitation, the Anti-Corn Law League was established in Manchester in 1838 (McCord, 1958, pp.15-16). Supporters of this movement were usually careful to distinguish it from Chartism, from which it was largely held aloof as a predominantly middle class single issue pressure group which they were keen would not be distracted from the singular aim of the immediate and total repeal of the protectionist

Corn Laws (McCord, 1958, pp.34-42). The scientific basis for its position rested with political economy, but league leaders were keen to moralize the appeal of the free trade ideal and portray it as above criticism of brash middle class self-interest. It was argued by advocates such as Richard Cobden that repeal and the consequent decline in bread prices through the importation of wheat would benefit all, and that the advance of free trade would enhance the prospects of international peace (McCord, 1958, pp.28-33). Unsurprisingly, the solemnization of meetings was often conducted by nonconformist preachers. For many supporters, in fact, the anticipated benefit of cheaper bread was lower wage costs (Gregg, 1984, pp.157-162) and the eventual repeal of the Corn Laws in 1846 was seen as a political triumph for the industrial middle classes.

Meanwhile, there had been attempts to heal the breach between the middle and working classes. One such endeavour was through the Complete Suffrage Union (1842 – 1844), set up by the Quaker Joseph Sturge. Although a predominantly middle class dissenting organisation, it intended to draw together radical members of the Anti-Corn Law League and moderate 'moral force' Chartists (McCord, 1958, pp.111-116, p.131 & p.132; Cowherd, 1959, Ch.8; Gregg, 1984, p.218; Spencer, 1904, Vol.1, pp.218-219). The organisation was based in the midlands, a region where the class divide in towns of small workshops, petty capitalists and craftsmen was less pronounced than in some northern towns dominated by large manufacturers (Read, 1964, Ch.2). Yet mutual suspicion between the factions prevailed and the organisation consequently disbanded. A young middle class local delegate in the negotiations named Herbert Spencer found the Chartist representatives to be 'fanatics' who 'would listen to no compromise' (Spencer, 1904, Vol.1, p.219).

From the 1830s, traditionalists within the established Church were experiencing religious orthodoxy being seriously assailed by modernizing influences. The 'adherence' of the lower orders had been eroded with the breakdown of paternal relations (Perkin, 1972, Ch.6). In some areas of the north, dissenters were outnumbering those of Anglican persuasion (Cowherd, 1959, p.16 & pp.67-68; McLeod, 1996, pp.27-29, each for 1851 census estimates). Middle class dissent surfaced in campaigns against the payment of Church rates through the Church Rate Abolition Society, founded in 1836, and pressure for the disestablishment of the Church through the Anti-Church State Association, which was founded in 1844 (Cowherd, 1959, Ch.12).

The battle between traditionalists and modernizers was keenly fought out in education. But just who were the modernizers here? Very modest beginnings of state funding of education had been introduced in 1834 (Cowherd, 1959, pp.117-118). In defence of their own schools, often as dissenting academies, and of their religious liberty, dissenters initially favoured a level playing field of state funding. However, they came to oppose state funding in the fear that state involvement would extend education in the direction of the realignment of the working class outlook toward that of the Anglican establishment (Cowherd, 1959, Ch.3). On the other hand, Anglicans were fearful of the secular educational emphasis and competitive spirit associated with utilitarianism, and Perkin (1972, pp.290-308) has suggested that sections of the middle classes were favourable to the extension of education to the working class, but only so long as it was under middle class guidance. These and other fears, such as potential pressures on wages and the possibility that the working class might acquire ideas 'above their station', as well as opposition from the middle classes to their taxation for the education of working class children when already providing for the education of their own, delayed the expansion of state education to the detriment of the English working class. Whilst radicals attacking the privileges of the landed elite, the same dissenting and entrepreneurial middle classes were often far more conservative on the issues of divesting political power and extending education to the working class.

The impact of science offered a further challenge to religious traditionalists. Interest in science advanced from the early Victorian period as witnessed through an increase in scientific periodicals. Demonstrations of applied science and new inventions and gadgets were of great interest to the general public (Johnston, in Dennis & Skilton ed., 1987, pp.110-114). Biology and geology had made substantial progress during the early nineteenth century (Somervell, 1929, pp.126-129) and the developments in the latter refuted widely held creationist views of history based on a literal interpretation of biblical teachings. They showed that the world had not been 'created' in 4004 B.C., but had an immensely more lengthy history of gradual change. Such findings would come to maturity around the mid-century in the evolutionism of Darwin, Spencer and others. The agnosticism of Spencer's evolutionism was in fact a secularized and systematized product of middle class dissent. It portrayed the triumph of free enterprise capitalism as an advanced stage in the laws of natural change.

To the established Church, the prospect of other worldly paradise or eternal damnation as the reward or punishment respectively for this-worldly behaviour remained firmly emphasised. Evangelism experienced a revival during the early nineteenth century, peaking around the time of the first Reform Act. Sometimes the chosen religion of paternalistic aristocrats who held a favourable attitude toward the old order, it placed greater emphasis on the mitigation of misery in this world through humanitarian social intervention. Combined with the interventionist secular social philosophy of utilitarianism, aristocracy and Church faced reformist pressures from within (by Evangelism) and attack from outside (by utilitarianism) (Perkin, 1972, pp.284-290). Utilitarianism, along with laissez faire, challenged the old order by basing social reforms on the democratic principle common to Enlightenment theories of promoting the greatest happiness to the greatest number.

Utilitarianism and laissez faire liberalism, the latter essentially referring to government non-intervention in economic matters, began as virtually indistinguishable philosophies of the rising middle class, having a common root in the ideas of political economy. Both emphasised the importance of free market forces and minimum and efficient government to replace outmoded, irrational and inefficient traditions and ceremonies, but they came to part in their triumph (Perkin, 1972, pp.252-270).

Utilitarianism emphasised the need for rational progress through the systematic modernization of legislation and institutions. Its quest for social efficiency rested on the materialist philosophy that social institutions could be designed on the premise that pain avoidance and pleasure seeking governed human behaviour. New social institutions could provide the basis for modifying behaviour to enhance self-support with the aim of relieving pressure on the rates. With this purpose in mind, and with significant middle class support, the harsh legislation of the Poor Law Reforms and the workhouse test were introduced in 1834.

Its public servant advocates favoured an accumulation of piecemeal reforms to tackle particular social problem areas. According to Kitson Clark (1967, Ch.8), the humanitarian and liberal conscience of public opinion supported piecemeal intervention to alleviate the dire working and living conditions that unbridled capitalism had delivered to so many. Beginning with the factory legislation of 1833, Chadwick and other public servants conducted systematic research into problematic social conditions, such as the state of public health amidst squalid urban conditions, providing material for official reports and new legislation. Policing the legislation then went hand in hand with the feedback of improved social information which became the basis for further investigation, reports and legislative intervention (Kitson Clark, 1967, Ch.8). By such means, it is argued that the modern state grew unintentionally and ad hoc through a process of cumulative piecemeal reforms.

From the 1830s, government officials had access to improved social statistics, provided, for example, by employers, local authorities and the police (Abrams, 1968, Ch.3). Utilitarian minded public servants became increasingly involved in attempts to remedy undesirable social conditions that they had factual evidence of through the mechanism of government. They came to emphasise administrative efficiency above humanitarianism or paternalism and interventionism rather than laissez faire as the means to achieve happiness maximization. In this form, they often drew condemnation from supporters of entrepreneurialism and represented the ideal of an emerging professional middle class whose value was promoted less in free market terms and more in terms of their expertise which was argued to be necessary for the smooth running of society (Perkin, 1972, Chs.7 & 8). In 1850, Herbert Spencer, a representative of the laissez faire camp, directed arguments in his first major work, Social Statics (1970), against both aristocratic privilege and paternalism and utilitarian intervention.

Laissez faire, whilst firmly in the tradition of political economy, was more radically non-interventionist, as even the political economists appreciated a need for the role of the state in the provision of certain public utilities and for national defence. A potent economic ideal of the entrepreneurial middle class, laissez faire strongly encompassed the moral ideal of 'self-help', promoted in 1859 by Samuel Smiles in a publication by that name (Fielden, 1968). But whether the type of radical liberalism that laissez faire embraced ever became a characteristic ideology or practice of Victorian England is highly questioned (for example by Watson, 1973; Rayner, 1962; Brebner, 1948). The abolition of the Corn Laws has often been taken as heralding an era of non-intervention and free trade. But whilst a triumph against the restrictive practices benefiting the landed interests, this reform had already been preceded by an accumulation of interventionist reforms sponsored by Evangelists, paternalistic Tories and utilitarians, offering some protection to the working classes against the most unscrupulous employers and squalid conditions of urban life. Whilst utilitarians had sided with supporters of laissez faire against landed interests, they came to increasingly embrace interventionism where the facts of non-intervention showed that the misery of the many was a consequence of the happiness of a new wealthy few. Following such reasoning, a justification could even be made for a degree of redistribution of wealth and income by reference to the law of diminishing returns (Brinton, 1933, Ch.2)!

New universities, such as the Benthamite University College, London – opened in 1828 – and mechanics institutes etc. did take to science and were prepared to open their doors to dissenters (Gregg, 1984, pp.245-262). However, the traditional universities remained the bastions of education of the landed upper and upwardly mobile middle classes. They were usually reached through the public schools, required adherence to the established Church, and commonly resisted the teaching of science (Wiener, 1981, Ch.2). For Wiener, through lesser revolutionary change in

England, old order elites had made a partial accommodation to industry and commerce. Through this lack of a revolutionary break, elitist culture was carried well into the industrial period, and could be found effectively preserved within the institution of the public school. In the quest for their sons to avoid their own characterisation as 'philistine' by traditional elites, sections of the middle classes were increasingly using their industrial made wealth to gain access for their children to an education befitting gentlemanly status. Consequently, the public schools were expanding during the 1840s (Wiener, 1981, Ch.2). With Weberian overtones, Wiener has argued that these institutions helped to promote a counter-revolution of cultural attitudes amongst the emerging generations of the middle classes who were educated to hold science and industry in disdain. For Wiener (1981, Ch.8), the consequence of this conversion was a relative decline in England's economic performance. Conversely, it has been argued that many public schools were reformed to suit the growing middle class intake; they became more competitive and took a greater interest in science (Perkin, 1972, pp.290-308).

The latter half of the nineteenth century witnessed the further advance of interventionism and the growing scale of social institutions. Whilst part of an already cumulative process, interventionism also bore some relationship to extensions in the franchise and the competition of political parties for the mass vote (Rayner, 1962). The 1880s also saw the rise of collectivism and the institutionalization of industrial conflict with the spread of trade unions amongst unskilled workers. New professions had emerged emphasising the need for their members' expertise for the well-being of society (Perkin, 1989). The utilitarian emphasis of scientific intervention by professional experts became extended to the outlook of Fabian socialists. Local municipalisation and public utilities were expanded and state education had been introduced. The growth of joint stock companies provided access to far greater investment from the public, enabling the promotion of larger scale businesses which were becoming characteristic of this later stage of capitalist development. France and Germany had industrialized along interventionist lines and were closing the gap on Britain. This precipitated a rush to exploit the colonies (Hobsbawm, 1974, Ch.9) and growing international tensions.

Compared to Britain's economic dominance and a climate of optimism in the benefits of free trade during the mid-nineteenth century, this was a different world. The political philosophy of New Liberalism linked progress with interventionism, and evolutionism was used to support colonialism by social Darwinists (Kidd, 1894) and Fabians (Shaw, 1900). This was all anathema to such old school radical liberals as Herbert Spencer.

5 | Herbert Spencer
Life and Works

It is the intention in this chapter to review Spencer's life and works with an emphasis on their micro social context. Spencer's two volume Autobiography serves as an organizational framework. However, this source is not approached uncritically. Other material, including viewpoints from those who knew him well, is used to add an external discipline to Spencer's self-portrayal.

Spencer's background and major intellectual achievements
Herbert Spencer was born on 27 April, 1820, at 12 Exeter Row, Derby – a rapidly growing provincial town of small manufacturers and workshops. He was brought up in a lower middle class dissenting household during a period of radical middle class agitation. Educated largely within his family, both Spencer's educational experience and political socialization worked powerfully together to instil a social outlook which remained relatively unchanged throughout his life. Generalized from the self-image of moral rectitude of the dissenting entrepreneurial middle class, this outlook idealized an industrial society of self-supporting, self-motivated enlightened individuals.

In his 'Autobiography', Spencer provided evidence and speculation of considerable religious non-conformity in the lives of his predecessors (Spencer, 1904, Vol.1, Ch.1). It is suggested, although Spencer found it impossible to establish with certainty, that distant predecessors may have come to England from France as persecuted Huguenots (Spencer, 1904, Vol.1, pp.3-7). From the generation of his grandparents, though, there is clear evidence of Methodist persuasion and salient characteristics of reformism and individual fortitude and sobriety in an environment in which dissenters faced a degree of persecution (Spencer, 1904, Vol.1,

pp.7-42). Adopting a Lamarckian view of the inheritance of acquired characteristics, Spencer was clearly proud to feel that he had inherited such moral characteristics from his predecessors (Spencer, 1904, Vol.2, essay entitled Reflections).

The figures of greatest direct influence on Spencer appear to have been his father, George Spencer, and his uncle, the Reverend Thomas Spencer. George, a schoolmaster, was admired by Herbert for his inventive and artistic ability (Spencer, 1904, Vol.1, p.43). He became secretary of the Derby Philosophical Society (Spencer, 1904, Vol.1, p.87), a debating society founded by Erasmus Darwin (the grandfather of Charles Darwin) who had been involved in the renowned Birmingham Lunar Society. George had once ventured, unsuccessfully, into lace manufacture in Nottingham (Spencer, 1904, Vol.1, pp.68-69). He had no time for titles or gestures of salutation in social encounters (Spencer, 1904, Vol.1, p.47). George turned from Methodism, which he came to find a too hierarchical denomination, and later in life identified with the Quakers (Spencer, 1904, Vol.1, pp.82-83). He worked hard for self-improvement and the improvement of others, but overwork led to a breakdown in his health which left nervous irritability and depression in its wake (Spencer, 1904, Vol.1, p.55, pp.66-67), the main victim of which appeared to be his wife Harriet (Robertson, 1927, p.194).

Spencer's siblings all died when young. His father did not press his education, fearing that Herbert's constitution might not be rigorous enough for the demands (Spencer, 1904, Vol.1, p.67, p.71). He was against disciplinarianism and rote learning, and consequently Herbert's youth was comparatively unrestrained. He often wandered the surrounding Derbyshire countryside, drawing and collecting wild life specimens and his imagination was early absorbed in 'castle building' (Spencer, 1904, Vol.1, pp.71-77) – the daydreaming of schemes. As a boy he enjoyed fishing and on one occasion was saved from drowning by the bravery and presence of mind of a youngster named George Holme (Spencer, 1904, Vol.1, pp.73-74; Duncan, 1908, p.10). There transpired a long friendship and debt of gratitude (Duncan, 1908, p.10, p.378).

Whilst still at home, Spencer's own aversion for rote learning meant that he gained no formal education in English grammar and found the 'dead language' of Latin most trying because, he claimed, of the dogmatic form rather than reasoned understanding involved in its principles (Spencer, 1904, Vol.1, p.84, p.88). Spencer's early education was governed by a knowledge of things around him, especially an intimacy with nature, more than by book learning. Family discussions on religious, political, moral and scientific topics by his independent minded father and uncles had much impressed him (Spencer, 1904, Vol.1, pp.85-86). Access was available to a broad range of periodicals, and Herbert assisted his father in setting up scientific experiments for teaching purposes (Spencer, 1904, Vol.1, p.86). This latter environment Spencer attributed to his father's influence on his tendency to search for causes in all phenomena (Spencer, 1904, Vol.1, p.89). Overall, there existed a context of educational freedom, intellectual self-help, the pursuit of original thinking and a disregard for unquestioned human authority (Spencer, 1904, Vol.1, p.79).

Thomas Spencer had attended Cambridge and qualified for the priesthood, yet he remained a dedicated and outspoken reformist – this despite the fact that he would presumably have had to sign the Thirty-Nine Articles of allegiance to the Anglican Church. In religious matters, he followed the family antipathy for ritual and ceremony and favoured the ongoing Reformation of the Church to reduce the ceremonial content of its services. He worked hard to assist his parish community, was involved in the Complete Suffrage Movement, active in the Anti-Corn Law League whose meetings he blessed, against the provisions of the old Poor law, and was a strong advocate of temperance (Spencer, 1904, Vol.1, pp.27-30). When young Herbert was once asked at an evening party why he did not join in the dancing, Thomas retorted in puritanical fashion that "no Spencer ever dances" (Spencer, 1904, Vol.1, p.28).

From the age of thirteen to sixteen, Herbert Spencer was educated away from home under his uncle Thomas at the parsonage of Hinton Charterhouse, near Bath, where Thomas was the curate (Spencer, 1904, Vol.1, Ch.7). Arriving with his parents on the pretext of a holiday visit, Herbert was aggrieved at the deception when he realized that he was to stay and they were to return home (Spencer, 1904, Vol.1, p.12). Faced with the sterner academic regime of his uncle, dislike of a fellow pupil, and his own feeling of homesickness, Herbert shortly absconded home to Derby (Spencer, 1904, Vol.1, pp.95-97). He had calculated that about one hundred and fifteen miles were covered by foot in this journey taking just three days (Spencer, 1904, Vol.1, p.97)! Rebelliousness and the determination to see a difficult task through were characteristics clearly evident from a young age.

Spencer eventually settled down at Hinton, returning home to Derby mainly only for scheduled summer vacations. In his correspondence home, evidence emerged of occasional self-doubt as he tired in his studies and questioned his ability to retain his learning (Duncan, 1908, p.17). In response to the boy's concern, his father's analysis was that he did not sufficiently live in his subject – an ironic comment when viewed from the facts of Spencer's later life! Normally, however, the criticism was that Spencer had a too high regard for his own attainments (Duncan, 1908, p.17).

Whilst at Hinton, Spencer studied Euclid, algebra, trigonometry and chemistry. He became familiar with some of Newton's works and read Harriet Martineau's work popularizing political economy (Spencer, 1904, Vol.1, pp.102-110). His educational progress had been most noticeable in mathematics in which his uncle thought that he had outstanding ability (Duncan, 1908, p.14). Spencer retained an aversion for languages and grammar, although he made some effort to learn Latin, Greek and French (Spencer, 1904, Vol.1, p.108). Great joy accompanied his first appearance in print with an article on salt crystallization (Crystallization) in the Bath Magazine in January 1836 (Spencer, 1904, Vol.1, pp.111-112). This was soon followed by an article entitled The Poor Laws (March 1836) which used quotations from the scripture to support his arguments in favour of self-support through thrift and hard work.

Spencer completed his education having 'never passed an examination' (Spencer, 1904, Vol.1, p.336). He returned home in 1836. Undecided regarding his future vocation, he commenced teaching geometry during the summer of 1837 (Spencer, 1904, Vol.1, pp.121-123). Like his father, Spencer's methods were not mechanical or coercive and he claimed that his relationship with his students was a close one (Spencer, 1904, Vol.1, pp.121-123). The teaching lasted for only three months. In retrospect he believed that had he pursued teaching as a career, his methods would have found little favour with parents who would have likely preferred more dogmatic, rote-like and coercive methods to be applied (Spencer, 1904, Vol.1, p.124).

In 1837 Spencer begun, through a family connection, an engineering career in various aspects of railway building, which, though discontinuous, was to span about ten years (Spencer, 1904, Vol.1, Ch.9-12 & Ch.19-21; Duncan, 1908, Ch.3 & Ch.5). Assignments as surveyor, draftsman, bridge designer, works superintendent and locomotive tester enabled the utilization of his knowledge of mathematics, mechanics, geometry and drawing. This period was sprinkled with practical inventions and innovative improvements (Spencer, 1904, Vol.1, p.149-150, p.165) and the writing of journal articles on scientific and social matters. In a clerical post dealing with correspondence, Spencer made an effort to improve his spelling and grammar (Spencer, 1904, Vol.1, pp.158-160).

His absorption with nature as a child was now supplemented by frequent country walks with friends, and Spencer's interests in geology were furthered by his observations of railway cuttings and his gathering of fossil collections (Spencer, 1904, Vol.1, pp.175-176).

At the age of twenty, Spencer became acquainted, through reading Lyell, with Lamarck's naturalistic theory of biological change through use inheritance (Spencer, 1904, Vol.1, p.176). His defence of this view was clear in a later essay which challenged supernatural explanations of biological diversity (In Spencer, 1883a, essay entitled The Development Hypothesis). But the Lamarckian theory had broader implications for Spencer. It became extended to explain the modifiability of human nature through the inheritance of moral traits reinforced over generations by the social environment.

Although involved in railway engineering, Spencer had by his early twenties developed some germinal ideas on the scope of government and individual rights. Despite his naturalistic leanings, these ideas exhibited the influence of his uncle's religious strictures and keen sense of abstract justice. During a break in his railway employment in 1842, Spencer returned with his uncle to Hinton. As a pamphleteer in dissenting causes, Thomas had useful connections. His introduction of Herbert to the Reverend Edward Miall, editor of the 'Nonconformist', a journal of religious dissent and an organ of the Complete Suffrage Movement that Miall had established in 1841, resulted in the publication between June and December 1842 of a series of letters written by Spencer on social matters, entitled On the Proper Sphere of Government (Spencer, 1904, Vol.1, pp.207-212). In these letters, Spencer attempted to logically delineate a restricted role for the state from certain basic principles rather than from custom. One consequence was a callous disregard for the sufferings of the poor (Nonconformist, 1842, letter 4).

During 1842 and 1843, Spencer became involved in the Complete Suffrage Movement (headed by Joseph Sturge) which he proudly represented as the Derby local secretary (Spencer, 1904, Vol.1, pp.217-220). These were times of radical politics in England, and Spencer later referred to this period as his own 'indignation phase' (Duncan, 1908, p.42). He held some antagonism, though, toward Chartist participants whom he came to view as too fanatical and uncompromising for the intended reconciliation between middle class radicals and working class representatives to be effective (Spencer, 1904, Vol.1, pp.219-220).

As member of a Derby Debating Society and Literary and Scientific Society, Spencer now realized that he was heading toward a literary career, but the opportunity to throw himself into this vocation had to wait. He had learned through the bitter experience of a failed attempt at a writing campaign in London that, like inventing, a literary career risked great financial hardship (Spencer, 1904, Vol.1, Ch.16; Duncan, 1908, pp.38-45). In these areas, he later came to argue that justice required substantial patent and copyright protection (Spencer, 1970, Ch.11; Spencer, 1897, article entitled Views Concerning Copyright). Spencer viewed inventions and literary works as the products of an individual's labour. Only through protection of the product from exploitation by others prepared to make easy gain at the expense of its creator could individuals be encouraged to make the necessary commitments from which society would benefit.

Meanwhile, Spencer gained familiarity with the works of John Stuart Mill, Thomas Carlyle and Ralph Emerson, and further inventions were pursued (Spencer, 1904, Vol.1, Ch.17). A brief spell as sub-editor of 'The Pilot', a radical local newspaper of the Birmingham area with links with the Complete Suffrage Movement, ensued (Spencer, 1904, Vol.1, Ch.18). Spencer had been introduced by Joseph Sturge to the editor, James Wilson (Spencer, 1904, Vol.1, pp.247-248). A variety of leading articles were contributed, but a return to more lucrative railway surveying quickly followed (Spencer, 1904, Vol.1, Ch19).

Preparatory reading was continued and non-lucrative inventions pursued. Spencer came to realize that to persist in the career of railway engineer ran the danger of offence to superiors in the organizational structure, since for him truth must not be subordinated to considerations of authority. This realisation appeared to be substantiated in a letter sent from Spencer's employer to his father in which reference is made to the hope that 'the temptation of a mind trusting on its own strength will not be allowed to assail him' (Duncan, 1908, p.28). Spencer exhibited an independent mindedness and tendency to stand firm when convinced that he was right and others wrong, whatever their official position (Spencer, 1904, Vol.1, p.300). And given his moralistic background and outlook, Spencer's distaste for the unscrupulousness and greed associated with railway mania helped to decide the issue. Railway business 'morality' consisted of playing on investors' greed for profit by misrepresenting the nature of the project and the soundness of their investment to them (In Spencer, 1883b, essay entitled Railway Morals and Railway Policy). On a personal level, his hard-working uncle Thomas lost heavily in his inexperienced buying of such shares (Spencer, 1904, Vol.1, pp.325-326); an experience which made Thomas come to question his previously severe and simplistic equation of poverty with just deserts (Spencer, 1904, Vol.1, p.345).

To some acquaintances, Spencer was by the age of twenty-five giving rationalism undue priority over religion. His father had, without success, long ago attempted to solicit his innermost religious convictions (Duncan, pp.18-19) and a religious minded friend terminated his acquaintance (Spencer, 1904, Vol.1, Ch.20). Spencer was becoming preoccupied in developing a basis for morals not deriving from the will of God but resting on laws in the nature of things. An indication of his prevailing scientific outlook can be gleaned from a remark previously made to a friend that "the moral Euclid remained to be written" (Spencer, 1904, Vol.1, p.266).

The opportunity to devote more time to this task arose in 1848. Thomas Spencer had introduced his nephew to James Wilson (not the James Wilson who edited The Pilot (Spencer, 1904, Vol.1, p.329)), founder of 'The Economist' – a journal promoting the doctrine of laissez faire and closely associated with the Anti-Corn Law League (Spencer, 1904, Vol.1, pp.329-334). Showing his credentials in his essays On the Proper Sphere of Government, Spencer was offered the post of sub-editor under Thomas Hodgskin. This post was ideal for Spencer's requirements. From it he derived a modest income and was left sufficient time for the research and writing of his first major work, Social Statics, which was completed in 1850 (Spencer, 1904, Vol.1, pp.341-342). His preoccupation later in life for his reputation led Spencer to leave the anarchist Hodgskin's undoubted influence on his work unacknowledged, making only two fleeting references to Hodgskin in his lengthy two volume Autobiography.

In Social Statics, evolutionism was a vague notion, and deductive reasoning based on first principles of individual rights and justice remained related back to a God whose will was deduced to be for human happiness. For Spencer, the realization of the latter in the long term required social non-interventionism to enable the adaptation of human nature to a condition of enlightened individualism. This was effectively a statement of the survival of the fittest.

During 1851, Spencer came across the biologist Von Baer's formula for change from uniformity to multiformity in the structure of plants and animals (Spencer, 1904, Vol.1, pp.384-385). He now had a view of structural and functional change which he believed applied to all organisms, within which he included the social. This was a pointer to a formula for cosmic evolution, but the crucial step in its development was only taken six years later in an essay entitled Progress: its Law and Cause (In Spencer, 1883a).

The publication of Social Statics led to a number of eminent acquaintances, some with whom Spencer strongly disagreed. One was Thomas Carlyle whom he met in 1851 and found to be reactionary, despotic, argumentative, arrogant, and hardly warranting the title of philosopher (Spencer, 1904, Vol.1, pp.379-384)! Spencer had made some effort to study Auguste Comte's Positive Philosophy in its original French form without making much progress (Spencer, 1899, in Duncan, 1908, p.545). His mastery of French was not great and being himself essentially a deductive thinker, he did not pursue far works whose founding principles he disagreed with (Spencer, 1904, Vol.1, pp.253-254; Spencer, 1899, in Duncan, 1908, p.538). Further knowledge of Comte was gained with the assistance of his friends George Elliot and G.H.Lewes (Spencer, 1904, Vol.1, p.545) who were converts to Comte's early Positivism. By

1854, with the benefit of Harriet Martineau's translated and condensed version of Comte's Course of Positive Philosophy, Spencer was able to formulate more clearly his position against that of Comte (Spencer, 1904, Vol.1, p.445). A critical review of Comte's classification of the sciences appeared in an 1854 article entitled The Genesis of Science (Spencer, 1904, Vol.1, p.446; Duncan, 1908, p.74; Spencer, 1883a). Forever sensitive to any inference that he had been influenced in anything but a negative way by Comte's works (Spencer, 1904, Vol.1, pp.359-360 & pp.445-446 & Spencer 1899, in Duncan 1908, p.545) the articles Reasons for Dissenting from the Philosophy of M.Comte (In Spencer, 1878) and The Classification of the Sciences (In Spencer, 1878) would ten years later summarise his opposition to Comte's positivism.

Martineau's translation was also to prove instrumental in the meeting of the two men. In 1856, Spencer met Comte in Paris, the pretext of the visit being to pass on some proceeds from Comte's translated work (Spencer, 1904, Vol.1, p.492-493). Spencer was little impressed by Comte, referring to him in a letter to his mother (Duncan, 1908, p.82) as 'a very undignified little old man'.

The opportunity to leave the Economist and embark fully on a writing career had been taken in 1853. Uncle Thomas had worked himself to an early death and bequeathed Spencer £500 and with it the security needed to take the step (Spencer, 1904, Vol.1, p.415). However, launching into his new career brought with it ominous signs. An inability to settle anywhere for long followed recurring experiences of heart palpitations which Spencer thought derived from over exertions on a holiday in Switzerland (Spencer, 1904, Vol.1, pp.431-432). This great restlessness between 1854 and 1855, during which time he was writing the first version of his Principles of Psychology, eventually led to sleeplessness, nervous exhaustion and nervous breakdown (Spencer, 1904, Vol.1, pp.467-468). The following eighteen months, referred to by Spencer as eighteen lost months (Spencer, 1904, Vol.1, Ch.32), were a catalogue of holidays and visits to friends. Sleeplessness persisted and minor mental exertions led to relapses in which reading became virtually impossible. Social intercourse that might involve lively discussion or acrimony had to be avoided since it would almost certainly lead to sleeplessness (Spencer, 1904, Vol.1, pp.494-496). This vulnerability to insomnia, incapacity to work to a rigid regime, and need to avoid excitable encounters were to stay with Spencer even when he had otherwise 'recovered'.

Previous years had been productive in essay writing over a broad range of topics and phenomena. Reviewing these works for publication together in the first volume of Essays: Scientific, Political and Speculative in 1857 helped Spencer to consolidate his system of thinking (Spencer,

1904, Vol.1, Ch.33). That year he had reached his first clear formulation of his theory of evolution in his essay Progress: its Law and Cause (In Spencer, 1883a).

By 1858, the first outline of the future major evolutionary works of his synthetic doctrine, the System of Philosophy, later renamed the Synthetic Philosophy, was envisaged (Spencer, 1904, Vol.2, Ch.34. Early sketch, pp.15-16). This scheme anticipated a series of works which would apply his formula of evolution to all phenomena. For both health and financial reasons, its undertaking was delayed (Spencer, 1904, Vol.2, pp.31-33). Spencer's hours of work were now largely restricted to between 10.00 a.m. and 1.00 p.m. each day, the reading of other works was often extremely difficult and could only be attempted in small doses, and insomnia frequently incapacitated him from work. Judging from his letters home, he was becoming a hypochondriac (Spencer, 1904, Vol.2, p.73 & p.111 for example). Yet he was to commit most of the rest of his life to the completion of this vast programme.

Working under such handicaps, Spencer resorted to dictation to increase his output (Spencer, 1904, Vol.2, p.43) and could occasionally circumvent his reading problems by having someone read to him. Sleeping difficulties were somewhat reduced by warm baths and occasional use of opium. As well as visits home from London, where he resided in rented accommodation in the fashionable districts of Hyde Park (Spencer, 1904, Vol.2, p.84), Kensington Gardens (Spencer, 1904, Vol.2, p.134) and Lancaster Gate (Spencer, 1904, Vol.2, p.145), his work was broken up by regular visits made to Scotland to meet friends, take in scenic walks, and fish – the latter especially to help relax his overactive mind.

Spencer always maintained that his theory was based on a balance of deductive and inductive reasoning. This would appear to have set him an enormous task given the scope of his works. Yet he also claimed to exhibit a 'constitutional idleness' (Spencer, 1904, Vol.1, p.296) – a remarkable assertion given the enormity of his output – and confessed to a lack of extensive reading (Duncan, 1908, p.490). This was likely to have been more the case following his breakdown. In fact, as argued by Kardiner and Preble (1962), Spencer was essentially a deductive thinker. Induction was very secondary and orientated toward the verification of his theoretical scheme. A friendly quip from T.H.Huxley recognized this tendency. During a conversation on the topic of tragedy he remarked that "Spencer's idea of a tragedy is a deduction killed by a fact!" (Spencer, 1904, Vol.1, p.403). Beatrice Webb, who knew Spencer well late in his life, likened his existence to that of a spider spinning a web; in Spencer's case, the spinning of his evolutionary theory to catch appropriate facts (Webb, 1950, p.26). And Darwin felt that Spencer would have been a truly great thinker if his observational powers had been as great as his deductive powers (Duncan, 1908, p.125).

Spencer acknowledged the advance made by Darwin's theory of biological evolution through natural selection in the latter's landmark work Origin of the Species, 1859 (Spencer, 1904, Vol.2, p.50). However, later feeling that Darwin's reputation had distorted the public's perception of the priority of ideas on evolution to his own detriment, Spencer, in a clearly transparent comment of apparent modesty and good manners, referred in his Autobiography to Darwin's response to receiving a volume of his essays in 1858:

'The following is Mr. Darwin's acknowledgment:

No, it is not as follows; for on consideration I decide to omit it. Notwithstanding the complements it contains, which seemed to negative publication, I was about to quote it, because it dispels, more effectively than anything else can, a current error respecting the relation between Mr. Darwin's views and my own' (Spencer, 1904, Vol.2, pp.27-28).

Spencer suggested that Darwin had been incorrect to ignore Lamarck, and maintained that biological evolution could be subsumed within his own more extensive laws of cosmic evolution.

More candidly, regarding his First Principles (1946) which had been originally published in 1862, Spencer, in his Preface to the Fourth Edition in 1880 commented that there had:

'been very generally uttered and accepted the belief that this work, and the works following it, originated after, and resulted from, the special doctrine contained in Mr. Darwin's Origin of Species' (p.xxi).

Whilst acknowledging that First Principles touched briefly on specific processes illuminated by Darwin (p.xxii), Spencer was at pains to emphasise that:

'The essay on 'Progress: its Law and Cause', co-extensive in the theory it contains with Chapters XV., XVI., XVII., and XX. in Part II of this work, was first published in the Westminster Review for April 1857' (p.xxi).

For greater financial security, Spencer had proposed to issue his System of Philosophy (later the Synthetic Philosophy), by subscription.

For the amended scheme of 1860 (Spencer, 1904, Vol.2, Appendix A), First Principles was to comprise the first volume and provide a systematic overview of the evolutionary process that was operative across all phenomena, followed by the issuing of volumes in which this process would be analysed with reference to specific subject areas, leading finally to The Principles of Morality. Spencer felt that subscribers were forthcoming in sufficient numbers in Britain and, through the efforts of E.L.Youmans in the United States, to indicate that the venture would be worthwhile. As it turned out, his judgement of human nature on this matter was not sound. Defaulters were numerous (Spencer, 1904, Vol.2, pp.64-65) and it was only possible to continue the scheme with the aid of money left to him by the death of his uncle William in 1860 (Spencer, 1904, Vol.2, pp.63-64).

One consequence of his financial state, which remained precarious until the publication of his popular work The Study of Sociology in 1873, was Spencer's periodic disqualification from voting outside of London through lack of the requisite property qualification (Spencer, 1904, Vol.2, p.125). Nevertheless, even when qualified, he apparently only ever voted once, that being for the Liberal Party. Spencer's views were too dissenting for conventional politics. He was highly scathing of excessive government and the poor calibre of politicians, whom, like the average layman, he argued were largely unversed in social science and preoccupied with the pursuit of short term sectional interests.

Preferring the company of small gatherings of well-known friends to that of large formal meetings, Spencer partook, from November 1864, in an exclusive network of scientists which became known as the 'X Club' (MacLeod, 1970). This was an informal club of top calibre scientists based on friendships of many years standing. Meeting monthly, they exchanged scientific views and banter in the relaxed atmosphere of a club whose only rule was to have no rules.

Further financial losses threatened a cessation of Spencer's works in 1866 (Spencer, 1904, Vol.2, Ch.42). Hearing of this, J.S. Mill and Spencer's X Club friends rallied support and proposed a scheme to take 250 copies of his works (Spencer, 1904, Vol.2, pp.136-137). It appears that upon the death of his father that year Spencer was able to decline the offer (Spencer, 1904, Vol.2, p.137 & Appendix C). He meanwhile assisted in the care of his invalid mother who shortly herself died (Spencer, 1904, Vol.2, Ch.43). Youmans, an unceasing champion of his cause in the United States, had raised a testimonial of $7,000 and so arranged it (in the form of public securities made out in Spencer's name) that Spencer, despite his proudly independent nature, could hardly decline (Spencer, 1904, Vol.2, pp.140-142).

Despite all this, two volumes of Principles of Biology were published in 1867, but his health suffered a relapse (Spencer, 1904, Vol.2, Ch.45). With the aim of aiding recovery, a six week tour of Italy was undertaken in 1868 (Spencer, 1904, Vol.2, Ch.46). From this tour, Spencer's dissent from reverence for tradition and religious piety showed itself in his comments on the works of art of Rahpael and Michaelangelo. These works, he felt, tended to be normally appraised in an attitude of awe under the 'halo of piety' with technical defects, especially in terms of light and shade, which detracted from their correspondence to reality, overlooked. Spencer's criticism in his search for truth likeness or literal reality likeness in all things, coupled with his independent minded disregard for authority and the following of custom and convention made him a dissenter from the religious and aesthetic orthodoxy (Spencer, 1904, Vol.2, pp.188-195). He took a similar dry view of poetry, music and opera. These evaluations reflected Spencer's puritanical background, his agnostic and modernist viewpoint, his scientific education and his engineering outlook.

In 1868, Spencer was elected to the select Athenaeum Club. This was a much valued source of relaxation with friends and offered the facility of a library and a billiard room – both well utilised by Spencer (Duncan, 1908, pp.494-495).

Between 1868 and 1872, two volumes of the Principles of Psychology were produced (Spencer, 1904, Vol.2, Ch.47 & 48). Ward (1909) has suggested that since these volumes were developed from the single volume first published in 1855, they did not fit neatly in between the subsequently written Principles of Biology and Principles of Sociology.

One method of work at this time consisted of exercise in the form of rowing of the Serpentine or rackets, periodically interjected with dictation to his assistant David Duncan (Duncan, 1908, p.142). Spencer had meanwhile recognized the need for systematic classification of the wealth of information necessary for his sociological works. He devised a classificatory scheme based on his evolutionism. Material on different civilizations, notably mainly from travellers' accounts, was read, selected and organised by assistants under his guidance to form the empirical basis of his Principles of Sociology.

Spencer's own travels during this period included a visit to France in promotion of the International Scientific Series, to Ireland and Scotland for fishing, and to north Wales and Switzerland (Spencer, 1904, Vol.2, p.281 & pp.232-238).

Whilst material for his Principles of Sociology was being organized, Spencer was asked to produce an accessible sociological work for the International Scientific Series. Undertaken with some initial reluctance as a distraction of his precious energies from his major works (Spencer,

1904, Vol.2, pp.242-243; Duncan, 1908, pp.158-160), this work, The Study of Sociology, published in 1873 (the first chapter of which had previously appeared as the first article of the first edition of the Popular Science Monthly in May 1872), catered well for the perceived need to more broadly diffuse the view and elaborate the nature and difficulties of social science. It became a highly remunerative venture, both selling well and increasing the demand for Spencer's other works (Spencer, 1904, Vol.2, pp.254-255; Spencer, 1897, Article entitled Views Concerning Copyright). Additionally, this work dealt with issues preliminary to the more substantial work and enabled Spencer to clarify in his own mind some of the problems and issues in the field of sociology (Spencer, 1904, Vol.2, pp.253-254). Furthermore, he came to recognize deficiencies in the sociological data that he intended to use.

The Principles of Sociology was embarked on from 1874 and the first volume (comprising three parts) appeared in 1876. One upshot of this work was a dispute initiated by the anthropologist E.B.Tylor who claimed that Spencer's ideas on the origin of religion which made reference to the ghost theory owed a remarkable but unacknowledged resemblance to his own previous works. Tylor's article, Mr. Spencer's Principles of Sociology, (In Mind, Vol.2, April 1877, pp.141-156) sparked an exchange of letters which appeared in the July edition of Mind, with Spencer claiming to be able to trace his ideas back to his own essay on The Origin of Animal Worship, published in 1870 in the Fortnightly Review (In Spencer, 1878).

The first part of the second volume of The Principles of Sociology, on Ceremonial Institutions (Spencer, 1883c), later became published chapter by chapter in periodicals in England, the United States, France, Germany, Italy, Hungary and Russia. This was succeeded by the second part on Political Institutions, actually published as a separate volume (Spencer, 1885b). The final volume, comprising sections on Ecclesiastical Institutions (Spencer, 1885c), Professional Institutions, and Industrial Institutions, was not completed intact until 1896 (Spencer, 1975).

Spencer meanwhile came to believe that his assistants' compilations of materials would be worthy of publication in their own right for their broad educational value. The resulting eight volumes, complied by Duncan (4), Scheppig (2) and Collier (2), which comprised standard classification tables applied to the history of a variety of societies and illustrated by selective quotations, became entitled the Descriptive Sociology (Spencer, 1904, Vol.2, Ch.51).

Worries over his state of health were playing an increasing part in directing Spencer's output. From 1875, the assemblage of information for his future Autobiography was leisurely undertaken (Spencer, 1904, Vol.2, pp.284-286). And fearing that he may not live to complete his Principles of Morality, which was to be the climax of the Synthetic Philosophy and most important work for the guidance of behaviour, Spencer sketched his leading ideas in The Data of Ethics between 1878 and 1879 (Spencer, 1904, Vol.2, Ch.55). This was followed by a trip to Egypt which left a sullen impression of the millennia of poverty and suffering of the masses alongside the grandeur of the monuments to despotic rulers – features typical of his loathed militant social type (Spencer, 1904, Vol.2, pp.341-343).

At the age of sixty, Spencer compared his views with those elaborated earlier in his life. He claimed that his ideal of the future remained that optimistically laid down in such early works as Social Statics, but that the time of its realization was more remote than he had initially supposed (Spencer, 1904, Vol.2, pp.365-366). From within the confines of his evolutionary scheme, he peered out at a society which he saw as 'retrogressing' toward collectivism and felt that 'the "good time" is very far distant' (Spencer, 1904, Vol.2, p.369). In 1881, he was forced to end the Descriptive Sociology with the issuing of its eighth part and a deficit of £3,250 (Spencer, 1904, Vol.2, p.351). Exasperated by the perceived lack of maturity of the public, Spencer commented that 'the stupidity of the public passes all comprehension' (Spencer, 1904, Vol.2, p.350). Eventually, further works were resumed under the terms of Spencer's will and the project was finally wound up in 1934.

By the time of his visit to America in the autumn of 1882, Spencer's health had further deteriorated and he had to be shielded from interviews, speech making (bar one in which he warned his American audience of the dangers of over working) and any excitements (Spencer, 1904, Vol.2, pp.388-389, pp.402-403). Lucrative lectures were turned down and by the time of his return he suffered a severe deterioration in his health (Spencer, 1904, Vol.2, pp.408-409). There is evidence that the end of this year marked a watershed in Spencer's position on the land question. The publication of a work entitled Progress and Poverty by the American land reformer Henry George reminded English readers of the radical position favouring land nationalisation that Spencer had adopted on the question in Social Statics. In embarrassed response, Spencer attempted to maintain logical consistency with his early work whilst retracting from its radical implications. For George, this was a contemptible attempt by Spencer to maintain intellectual integrity by one who had sold out to the landowning class.

Spencer's subsequent writing was slow and spasmodic as he faced bouts of relapse and improvement in his health. The less demanding work of the two volumes of his 'Autobiography' was tackled from 1886 (Spencer, 1904, Vol.2, Note, p.5) and completed in 1889. Other output between 1882 and 1889 consisted of four essays which, initially published in Contemporary Review in 1884, became later published together as The Man Versus the State (In MacRae (ed), 1969, an edition which includes a further essay that was first published in 1891), the section on Ecclesiastical Institutions, which was completed in 1885 and comprised part of the final volume of The Principles of Sociology, and some other minor articles including exchanges in 1884 with Frederic Harrison, follower of Comte's religion of humanity, over the religion of the future.

Yet to finish his Synthetic Philosophy, Spencer's work on sociology and on morality had to be finished. Under the circumstances of declining health and advancing age, this must have now appeared a virtual impossibility. The task cannot have been helped by the bitterness which arose toward his old friend T.H.Huxley. In 1871, Spencer had cause to defend himself in his essay Specialized Administration (In Spencer, 1878) against what he regarded as misrepresentations of his views in Huxley's article Administrative Nihilism (In Huxley, 1893). The dispute was then conducted amicably (Spencer, 1904, Vol.2, p.232). However, between 1889 and 1890, Huxley had contributed articles to the Times and the Telegraph through which Spencer felt misrepresented to a broader public by a close friend who should have known better (Duncan, 1908, pp.329-337). Only in 1893, after Huxley's Romanes Lecture essay Evolution and Ethics did reconciliation occur.

Writing in1893, Spencer commented that

'I am impelled to maintain........this desire to continue the task I have undertaken. This architectonic instinct tyrannizes over me. Such more comfortable life as I might lead if I would cease altogether to tax myself, I decline to lead' (Spencer, 1904, Vol.2, p.454, in essay entitled Reflections).

The previously written Data of Ethics had now been utilised as the first part of Spencer's first volume on morality now named Principles of Ethics. The remaining five parts constituting the two volumes were completed between 1891 and 1893, but not in their sequential order in the volumes. Three years later, with The Principles of Sociology finally completed, Spencer's monumental scheme of intellectual 'castle building' was realized. His secretary, Walter Troughton, recorded the celebrated moment thus:

'Mr. Spencer was seventy-six years of age when he dictated to me the last words of 'Industrial Institutions', with the completion of which the Synthetic Philosophy was finished – to be precise it was on the 13 August, 1896. Rising slowly from his seat in the study at 64, Avenue Road, his face beaming with joy, he extended his hand across the table, and we shook hands on the auspicious event. "I have finished the task I have lived for" was all he said, and then resumed his seat. The elation was only momentary and his features quickly resumed their customary composure' (Troughton, quoted in Duncan, 1908, p.380).

Spencer's last years were marked by a painful recognition that the course of British history was turning away from the individual enlightenment that he associated with evolution. His attack against the drift toward collectivism and growing state regulation had been taken up in the 1880s in the articles of The Man Versus the State. Now, at the end of the century, a retrogression to militarism, which Spencer had long detected, was evident in Britain's involvement in the Boer War. Outspoken as he was against this 're-barbarization', there was sullen recognition, consistent with his own social philosophy, that ideas alone cannot halt a slide in the moral condition. His final articles were incorporated into Facts and Comments, which was published in 1902.

Having completed his Synthetic Philosophy and outlived the age of which it was a product, Spencer died on 8th December, 1903. His ashes were entombed at Highgate Cemetery (Duncan, pp.477-482).

Spencer from a more critical stance

William James (1911) has commented that such extremes of greatness and smallness as Spencer exhibited can have rarely resided in the same person. Clearly, his life was a great monument to individual fortitude. However, we need to penetrate the veil of his Autobiography to detect some of his less attractive characteristics.

Spencer's life was not entirely consistent with the principles laid down in his works. Prior to embarking on his System of Philosophy, Spencer seriously considered applying for a consular post in India in the anticipation of sufficient income and time to undertake his project. He did not obtain the testimonial he hoped for from J.S.Mill who dissuaded him of the idea (Spencer, 1904, Vol.2, pp.23-24). In this peculiar episode, Spencer's personal intentions were clearly at odds with his opposition in theory to state colonization (Spencer, 1842, letter 6, pp.634-635; Spencer, 1970, Ch.27). Likewise, his pursuits of fishing and shooting could be criticized as barbaric 'survivals' from the point of view of his theory.

His preoccupation with his reputation was not related to intellectual matters alone. Spencer was keen to distance himself from organizations or people that he felt could taint his public image. His virtual screening out in his Autobiography of the anarchist Hodgskin's undoubted influence at the time of writing Social Statics has already been mentioned. When later in life he supported the Liberty and Property Defence League, an organization representing status quo propertied interests, he did so covertly (Offer, 1983) despite having previously emphasised the importance to social outcomes of all people openly expressing their honestly held opinions (Spencer, 1970, p.475 (quoted in Ch.7 of this text), reiterated in Spencer, 1946, pp.101-102). And when Beatrice Potter, a sympathetic and supportive friend in his old age, became engaged to Fabian Sydney Webb in 1892, he decided that it would no longer be appropriate for her to act as his literary executor. He nevertheless agreed that she should assist behind the scenes (Webb, 1950, pp.28-33).

Haight (1969, p.120) refers to the selective evidence utilised by Spencer in his Autobiography regarding the priority of his ideas. More generally, forever defensive of his originality, the source of some of Spencer's ideas can be difficult to specify. His militant and industrial typology, first systematically utilised in The Principles of Sociology (Spencer, 1885a, Pt.2, Ch.10-11) is a case in point. It is uncertain whether he was familiar with the usage of this typology in the works of Saint Simon and Comte. However, it was in the tradition of the political economists. It would have been part of the culture of the Anti-Corn Law League. It may have related to discussions in the household of Spencer's youth. And we are told that as a youngster Spencer read a work on political economy by Harriet Martineau. But he never documented his intellectual debt for this typology.

Despite emphasising the scientific nature of his theory, his own approach has been criticised as falling short of the rigors of scientific method. The key criticism is that deduction overwhelms induction and that consequently mountains of facts are selectively supplied for the purpose of verification of his theory. Such is the criticism made by Brinton (1937) of Spencer for providing a long list of bad laws as a form of proof against state interventionism, as well as Harrison's comment in an acrimonious exchange with Spencer that the latter's theory of religion in his Descriptive Sociology rests on 'a pile of clippings made to order' (Harrison, 1885, cited in Eisen, 1968, p.46).

Spencer was highly sensitive to the charge that his system had changed over time, especially when it implied that this reflected a tendency later in life to ingratiate himself with the establishment (Duncan, 1908, p.328). The evidence on this is somewhat mixed. George's analysis of Spencer's retraction on the land question is well sustained and documented. Indeed, Spencer even went so far as withdrawing the original Social Statics from circulation in England and issuing in 1892 a reworked and condensed version (Spencer, 1910) which omitted the offending section on land nationalization. His call for the extension of the franchise also became a very qualified one, doubting the wisdom of its extension to the working class and to women. On the other hand, protestations against the Boer War (articles in Spencer, 1902) were hardly aimed to court the establishment. And as a matter of principle, or perhaps as his response to the lack of recognition from academia earlier in his life, Spencer declined most of the many academic honours proffered in his later years (Spencer, 1902, pp.233-234; Duncan, 1908, pp.168-170, pp.182-183, pp.233-236 & pp.588-589).

Given the great time span of his works, many of Spencer's views remained relatively fixed. Indeed, Ward (1909) has criticised Spencer for retaining the prejudices of his youth. The fixity of Spencer's position is evident when comparing his anti-state posture in his Man Versus the State essays, first published in the 1880s, with that of Social Statics, first published in 1850. The growing tone of pessimism against the extension of the state and the advance of collectivism, which marked his later works, arguably indicated the existence of fixed principles applied to changed social conditions. A number of factors contributed to this fixity. One was certainly the early and powerful complementary effect of his family socialization and education on his mind set. Although the religious connotations of his early works eventually disappeared, the associated laissez faire view of justice expounded in his very earliest essays always remained. In his frequent replies to criticisms, Spencer rarely acknowledged other than that he had been misrepresented or misunderstood. This process helped to entrench his position over a number of decades. Other factors conspired to work in the same direction. One was that his mind was closed in the deductive logic of his own scheme. Spencer admitted that he never persevered with works whose fundamental principles he disagreed with. Additionally, he developed a propensity for highly selective verification of his theory. Even evidence which seemed to refute it was used to show that society was going in the wrong direction rather than his theory possibly being incorrect.

The emphasis in his work of course changed over time. Social Statics and his other early essays were written in a climate of middle class optimism in free enterprise capitalism. It was utopianist and offered reassurance that society was moving in the right direction of possessive individualism. His Principles of Sociology was less utopianist. It aimed to provide a massive empirical base for the scientific verification of his laws of evolution. More cautiously, and with a degree of resignation, Spencer's last major work, The Principles of Ethics, aimed to provide a pragmatic benchmark for an appropriate morality for the present and the near future based on his now apparently scientifically established laws of evolution.

Spencer inherited a fragile nervous system. His excessive egoism and will power led to a life that seriously damaged his nervous constitution. What were the motives that kept him to his demanding intellectual task despite his ailing health? Spencer documented these as including his propensity for systems building, the quest for honour (despite declining many formal academic honours) associated with great achievement, and the desire to effect men's actions through the diffusion of truth (Spencer, Reflections, in Spencer, 1904, Vol.2).

In some of his later works, such as the Man Versus the State essays, Spencer gave a gloomy warning against both Toryism and impending socialism. But the pessimistic tone of the warning raises the issue of the futility of Spencer's entire output. This relates to Spencer's opposition to ontological idealism. For Spencer, ideas were not the driving force of social change and would only be acceptable if they reflected the prevailing moral condition. It would therefore appear that if society were retrogressing, his own arguments could have little effect, and if society were progressing there would be little need for his theory!

Prophets of Progress: Saint Simon, Comte and Spencer

6 | Herbert Spencer
View of History

In this chapter, the author will show how Spencer viewed history from his evolutionary perspective and view of progress. It will be emphasised that these theoretical constructs for the interpretation of history were built around a dissenting middle class outlook which opposed upper class traditionalism and later became more preoccupied with challenging working class radicalism. Furthermore, it will be show that from the vantage point of the mid-nineteenth century English entrepreneurial middle class, Spencer's view of history held different implications form the French positivists Saint Simon and Comte. Reference will inevitably be made to Spencer's evolution and view of progress as templates for historical interpretation. In the following chapter, the author will take a more technical view of Spencer's laws of change and his 'enlightened' view of social phenomena.

Evolution, progress and history
Evolution for Spencer became expressed in a scientific formula for change applicable to all phenomena. He viewed society as like an organism, often taking the analogy to great lengths. Spencer argued that a scientific approach to history should be analogous to that appropriate to a biological organism (Spencer, 1885a, Vol.1, Pt.2, Chs.1-9; Spencer, 1883a, essay entitled The Social Organism). In the individual organism, the natural process of growth followed predicted structural and functional changes. This outlook Spencer took from Von Baer's formula for biological growth and Spencer claimed that like laws of natural change applied to the social organism. In both cases, the natural pattern of growth followed an advance in structural and functional complexity and sophistication. Just as the science of biology was not concerned with the biographical details of an individual's life, so the science of society should not be preoccupied with the details of historical events. In particular, history which focussed on the deeds of great men, battles, kings and queens and court intrigues was of little relevance to understanding morphological changes in society. To Spencer, such a preoccupation the product of a barbaric mentality which worshipped the use of power. It was the survival of a mentality from militant times and provided little information upon which to build

social laws with predictive value (Spencer, 1880, p183; Spencer, 1902, article entitled Spontaneous Reform; Spencer, 1904, Vol.2, p.253).

Spencer's social evolution claimed to be a science of natural history. As such, it applied to societies in ensemble and provided a scale against which the stage of evolution of any society could be set. However, Spencer did not maintain that a unilinear trajectory of change would necessarily be followed by each specific society. Rather, the grand course of evolution was a tendency from which individual societies may sometimes depart according to the broader environmental conditions that were at play. Nevertheless, like Saint Simon's and Comte's laws of progress, Spencer's evolution was claimed to be of universal validity and thus formulated above generalization from the history of a specific society. It is central to this thesis that none of these theories lived up to the latter claim. The characteristics of Spencer's social evolution, and his militant and industrial scale of progress, were derived from his view of English modernization from a position of mid-nineteenth century middle class dissent and entrepreneurialism. He used evolution from this viewpoint to interpret history and project his image of a future utopia – a social apex of small scale free private enterprise and a moral condition of enlightened individualism.

Unlike the French historical circumstances that weighed on Saint Simon and Comte, Spencer was not living in a society which had recently undergone dramatic social and political revolution. He did not share their intense experience of social loss and the need to recover aspects of the past in a future social order. Compared to France, in England, feudalism was in early decline, royal absolutism had been of limited intensity and duration, and social reform in the direction of the extension of individual religious, political and economic freedoms had been relatively gradual. These reforms had reached an advanced stage by the mid-nineteenth century with the rising power of the entrepreneurial and dissenting middle class. Spencer's family background reflected the outlook of this class. In his early works, Spencer felt in tune with these forces in a society that had already industrialised. As a spokesman for free enterprise, his theory of natural history, based on a class view of English history, emphasised the gradual extension of individual freedoms and rights through a progressive release of the individual from antiquated traditional constraints toward the logical conclusion of a free enterprise utopia (Delineated in Spencer, 1970) – social growth to the industrial society.

To complicate matters, alongside evolutionary growth, Spencer also interpreted history in terms of the more evaluative concept of progress. Leading to the same future utopia, his scale of progress utilized the militant and industrial typology. These were ideal types which bore the mark of political economy. In their purest form, they represented contrasting social patterns. Social reality always constituted a mix, but the pure types allowed the measurement of change as progressive or retrogressive. In Spencer's hands, the types differed in their constitution and evaluation from Saint Simon's like named terms.

For Spencer, militant societies exhibited a highly regimented form of social organisation, whereas the pure industrial type provided the social context for the maximisation of individual freedom, characteristics in common with the high point of social evolution which related to the structural and functional features of the advance of social complexity and specialization.

However, any view that Spencer meant that the advance of industry alone would inevitably lead to a society of freely associative individuals is based on a fundamental misunderstanding that the terminology can lead to. For Spencer, the militant and industrial scale is essentially a social typology. Thus, the social regimentation associated with past militant societies can re-emerge in the context of conflict between industrially advanced nations. Social progress is therefore more capable than evolution of reversal (retrogression) and can distort the natural evolutionary process.

Materialism versus idealism

Comte and Saint Simon were ontological idealists. Their social theories explained social change, instability and social order as determined by changing systems of thinking. For them, morality referred to the social condition external to the individual and was determined by the nature of the prevailing social dogma. Spencer opposed idealism and maintained that sustainable social change and the acceptance of ideas were determined by the malleable condition of man's moral nature. Furthermore, the moral condition was viewed in terms of the internal makeup of individuals. Its state was only gradually modifiable by the cumulative impact of the external social environment, but ultimately determined the range of social institutions upon which social order was possible. This is a materialist view of history in which appropriate modes of thinking and dominant institutions reflected the prevailing moral condition. History repeatedly illustrated, claimed Spencer, that no social dogma or institutions, however rationally constructed, could be imposed on man of unfit moral nature and expected to endure (Spencer, 1970, pp.238-246). Whilst social evolution indicated the advance of individual freedoms and rights, it was only compatible with social order at a pace of change limited by gradual changes in man's moral makeup in the direction of enlightened individualism. Furthermore, later in life, Spencer increasingly felt the tide of history to be running counter to this outcome with the social condition retrogressing in a growing climate of militancy amongst leading industrialised European societies. He came to despair that however rationally constructed he felt his evolutionary scheme and ethics of the future to be, such reasoning would have little effect if the general moral condition was retrogressing and was not conducive to receiving it (Spencer, 1904, Vol.2, Ch.59).

A framework for interpreting the past

For Spencer, evolutionary science required the tracing of changes in phenomena from its earliest detectable appearance (established in Spencer, 1946, specified on pp.246-247). In social phenomena, this meant tracing structural and functional changes from the most 'primitive' groupings up to advanced industrial societies. But how could we know the history of such a primitive past? The benchmark of natural evolution offered a convenient way out. Measured by its universal criteria, actual societies had reached various stages. Those remaining at a primitive stage on the scale corresponded to the historically primitive and were amenable to contemporary study. This offered Spencer, whose education in history was by his own admission limited (Spencer, 1904, Vol.1, p.115), apparent insight into the distant past of advanced societies which required little historical verification. It could be supported by evidence from travellers and explorers (Spencer, 1904, Vol.2, p.225), allowing Spencer, despite the questionable quality of the evidence, to substitute the role of armchair anthropologist for historian.

Spencer was aware of great interpretive difficulties in the reconstruction of man's distant past, acknowledging that the 'primitive' outlook would be entirely alien to us. However, he claimed that man's enduring rationality rendered its reconstruction possible. Our knowledge of principles of intellectual association in the classification of objects and processes allowed a rational reconstruction of man's outlook if environmental circumstances, including the infancy of scientific knowledge, were sufficiently specified to take account of. (Spencer, 1885a, Vol.1, pt.1, pp.96-100).

According to Spencer's evolutionary criteria, primitive societies were small and relatively structure-less and homogeneous groupings (Spencer, 1885a, Vol.1, p.459; Spencer, 1946, pp.382-384). They exhibited a limited division of labour or social hierarchy and a minimal regulatory apparatus, and conduct was governed mainly by custom and ceremony (Spencer, 1883c, Vol.2, Pt.4, Ch.1). Ritual and ceremony related to primitive religious notions. Spencer explained the origin of religion in terms of the 'ghost theory' (Spencer, 1885a, Vol.1, Pt.1). This theory emphasised that primitives lacked scientific understanding of much phenomena, including the experience of dreams. It was natural that dream experiences indicated to them a duality – a spirit which could leave the physical body, as it apparently did during the dream state, and return. From this, it was believed that the spirit could also live in a spirit world after physical death. Events unexplained by the underdeveloped state of science could be referred to the influence of spirits. Their believed intervention for good or ill gave rise to the need for propitiatory rites to placate them.

Spencer acknowledged that primitive societies in an evolutionary sense may have survived in an environment of peaceful coexistence (Spencer, 1885a, Vol.1, pp.509-510, pp.552-553; Spencer, 1885b, Vol.2, Pt.5, pp.234-235, pp.628-632; Spencer, 1978, Vols.1 & 2), thus rather awkwardly classifying them as a primitive form of the industrial social type. The militant social type emerged under circumstances of conflict between primitive groupings. With very limited productive techniques, success in battle was a matter of survival or the main source of supplementing wealth. Under such circumstances, groups best organized for warfare had a survival advantage over others (Spencer, 1885b, Vol.2, Pt.5, pp.569-571). A warlike external posture necessitated internal regimentation with survival value attached to the subordination of all areas of life to the requirements of warfare (Spencer, 1885b, Vol.2, Pt.5, Ch.17). Persistent conflict moulded, through the inheritance of acquired characteristics, the moral nature of successive generations to a callous disregard for the consequences to others of self-gratifying barbaric behaviour. This moral condition compounded the need for strongly imposed social regulation of the individual for society to cohere.

'Might is right' was an appropriate moral outlook under conditions of militancy. It permeated all areas of life and shaped the psychological traits of worship of and obedience to authority which were necessary to condition callous egoism to the social state. Insubordination was amongst the greatest of crimes, against which punishment took the form of severe retribution. Political control was despotic. Religion, which took the form of ancestor worship, was conflated with the political realm to project the fear of great rulers. Viewed as apotheosized (the transmutation from human to god) spirits of past rulers, the gods were vengeful and required the performance of propitiatory observances. Leaders, as blood relatives of past heroic and apotheosized rulers, held great religious as well a political sanction.

Through conflict, Spencer claimed that militant societies grew in size and evolved by a process of compounding, advancing in the complexity of their ceremonies and regulations, and subordinating the lives of individuals to the struggle for survival and expansion (Spencer, 1885a,

Vol.1, pp.507-521). These characteristics reached their height in militant early slave civilizations, for example in ancient Egypt and the Roman Empire. Populations were separated into ranks with details of appropriate behaviour heavily prescribed. Political and military organisation were inseparable, with power concentrated in the hands of a despot or an oligarchy (Spencer, 1885b, Vol.2, Pt.5, Chs.6-7). For Spencer, medieval societies still bore the marks of militarism. Trade and economic life were regulated and taxed for military purposes. Industrial pursuits were not held in high esteem. Social honour was attached to grandiose lifestyle and landed wealth which had been acquired through force of arms. Society formed a rigid hierarchical order of estates which was sanctified by religious ceremony and dogma.

To Spencer, much of human history has been a record of man's brutal nature appropriate to and shaped by the conflicts and struggles of a militant environment. Man would always be motivated by the pursuit of gratification, but the type of gratification and the means to its achievement were adaptations to survival in given conditions (Spencer, 1978, Vol.1, Ch.10). In militant societies, many suffered for the gratification of the powerful few. To powerful leaders, grand and lasting monuments were built through forced labour to endure as symbols of the use of coercive power and inspirations of an attitude of awe (Spencer, 1904, Vol.2, Ch.57). Views of history and society were typically couched in terms of legends of great leaders' heroic deeds and of divine intervention (Spencer, 1975, Vol.3, Pt.7, Ch.5). Likewise, the lavish splendour and display of medieval art and architecture, which Spencer referred to as 'barbaric art' (Spencer, 1902), was designed, at the expense of technical defect, to overpower the mind of the populace.

The notion of survival of the fittest was for Spencer relative to changing conditions. He strongly objected to the suggestion that his evolutionism equated it everlastingly with triumph through brute force (For example in Spencer 1897, article entitled M. de Laveleye's Error, pp.106-108). The struggle between societies had for much of history been beneficial to human evolution in conditioning recalcitrant man to social discipline. Under such conditions, the individual existed for the benefit of society. But militancy had assisted the evolutionary process of compounding and expanding societies. Evolutionary growth brought social differentiation and integration. In occupational and technological terms, it assisted the advance of specialized skills and industrial techniques in an increasingly integrated market (Spencer, 1946, pp.310-311). The more specialized the worker, the more he was an efficient producer and a consumer of other's products and services. Enhanced efficiency of production in response to growing consumer needs facilitated free market relations and spelt the demise of estate stratification based on inherited landed wealth, power and privilege. In place of the latter, in the emerging industrial society, income from the free market would increasingly become a measure of reward for effort and ability and a source of prestige that was open to individual achievement.

Spencer emphasised that a vital factor in this process of change remained the nature of relationships between societies. If international hostilities persisted, industry may advance but social relationships would remain regulated to the needs of conflict. The advance of industry provided no guarantee against reversion to militancy between and within societies. Under such conditions, the free market would not operate, protectionist economic policies would prevail, and resources would be siphoned by the state for destructive purposes. The full benefit of industrial wealth and free international trade, Spencer argued, required peace and security. The deregulated industrial type would thus first emerge in a society best placed to allow the development of individual freedoms which accompanied peaceful coexistence.

England at the forefront

In England, from Spencer's viewpoint, centuries of relative peace had helped avoid the centralizing features of the more militant European societies. Military leadership had become subordinated to political leadership and society had reformed in the direction of political, religious and economic freedoms. These conditions were conducive to the first social metamorphosis from the regulated militant toward the free enterprise industrial society through the growing social ascendency of the entrepreneurial middle class.

In the fully developed industrial society, coercive regulatory apparatus would wither away. Individual freedoms would be restricted only by the requirement of all to obey the non-infringement of the equal freedom of other individuals (Spencer, 1970, p.68). This future social state would require the moral condition of enlightened individualism. Spencer was at pains to point out that given man's ingrained moral condition under militancy, enlightened individualism could only be the outcome of a long process of moral refashioning through gradual social reform accompanying peaceful relations between nations.

France's relative economic backwardness related to her social and moral heritage. Her feudal tradition, royal absolutism, state centralism and Catholic intolerance and grandeur were all for Spencer features of militancy. Those French social theorists who adopted a position of ontological idealism and looked forward to regulated utopias were mistaken. Comte's positivism was a case in point on both counts (In

Spencer, 1878, Vol.3, essay entitled Reasons for Dissenting from the Philosophy of M. Comte). The institution of the positivist dogma would not itself solve the French crisis of social and political instability because, Spencer argued, the crisis was not essentially an intellectual one. Instability in post-Revolution France derived not from the lack of a stabilizing dogma but from attempts to institute a libertarian political system ahead of its corresponding moral state. In consequence, the French were only too prepared to deliver themselves to state regulation under the dictatorship of Napoleon following the anarchy which accompanied the newly acquired freedoms of the Revolution (In Spencer, 1878, Vol.3, essay entitled Reasons for Dissenting from the Philosophy of M. Comte). As Spencer later stated:

'The defective natures of citizens will show themselves in the bad acting of whatever social structure they are arranged into. There is no political alchemy by which you can get golden conduct out of leaden instincts' (In MacRae (ed.), 1969, Spencer, essay entitled The Coming Slavery, p.110).

A recent history of retrogression
Even in England, there remained a mixture of militant and industrial social characteristics (Spencer, 1885a, Vol.1, pp.567-575) which for Spencer evidenced the gradual nature of change. In his first major work, Social Statics, Spencer launched his main attack on aristocratic privileges as remnants of militancy. At this stage in his thinking, he opposed absolute property rights in land which he viewed as God's bequest to mankind. Existing patterns of land ownership were the outcome of past acquisition by force under conditions of militancy. Justice therefore required that land should be turned over to social ownership (Spencer, 1970, Ch9).

Despite evolutionary change and industrial development, for Spencer there always existed the possibility of social retrogression toward militancy. Spencer's concern with retrogressive tendencies later shifted toward the growing collective power and influence of the working class. The militant and industrial typology allowed comparisons to be made between practices traditional to such 'less advanced' countries as India and the English working class (Burrow, 1968, pp.240-241). For Spencer, governments held no intrinsic power. They were only instruments of social power and often operated highly inefficiently in complex modern societies. Yet, despite evidence to the contrary, he detected in the working class a widespread belief in the ability of governments to have some type of magical power of their own to create something from nothing. This he saw as an illusory faith and the 'survival' of a militant mentality (In Spencer, 1883b, essay entitled Parliamentary Reform: the Dangers and the Safeguards). It was comparable to the continuing primitive faith that idol worshippers had in the powers of their idol to work desired effects despite repeated contrary evidence (In Spencer, 1878, Vol.3, essay entitled Political Fetichism, & in MacRae (ed.), 1969, Spencer essay entitled The Sins of Legislators). It indicated both an underdeveloped social scientific outlook and a moral immaturity in the resignation of individual responsibilities to other supposed forces. Fearful of the consequences of growing working class power, by 1860 Spencer came to argue that to check this retrogressive belief in state power, the vote should only be extended to where a link was established between outlay to – in the form of direct taxation – and benefit from the provisions of public authorities (In Spencer, 1883b, essay entitled Parliamentary Reform: the Dangers and the Safeguards).

A growing conservatism can also be traced in Spencer's thinking regarding the political influence of women. In Social Statics (1970, pp.169-171), Spencer advocated women's enfranchisement. He was also critical of the use of coercive power over women by men. By the time he published The Study of Sociology, Spencer left the question of extending the political influence of women unanswered, but his portrayal of female psychology strongly implied the negative (Spencer, 1880, pp.369-377). By the time that The Principles of Sociology started to be published, the negative was asserted and the traditional housewife role advocated (Spencer, 1885a, Vol.1, pp.755-758).

From a position of youthful radicalism optimistic of future progress, Spencer was arguably later in life becoming pessimistic and conservative, a key theme identified by Wiltshire (1978). Spencer claimed that the shift was in society which he analysed as retrogressing, against which checks needed to be put in place. In 1876, his periodization of recent British history placed a watershed at approximately 1850 (Spencer, 1885a, Vol.1, Pt.2, Ch.11) when Social Statics had been published. Previous decades following the defeat of Napoleon in 1815 had witnessed the progress of industry, peace and individual freedoms. Decades subsequent to 1850 evidenced retrogression in the form of growing state intervention and military posturing. During the 1880s, he traced what he saw as the Liberal Party's betrayal of its earlier defence of individual liberty in favour of interventionism (MacRae (ed.), 1969, Spencer, essay entitled The New Toryism) and referred to a growth of trade union 'tyranny of organization' as militancy related to industrial conflict (MacRae (ed.), 1969, Spencer, essay entitled The Coming Slavery, pp.106-107). In trade unions he perceived a growing tendency of workers to give up their individual rights to despotic organisations and use organised might to attain collective benefits for themselves at the expense of other individuals. Spencer feared that the extension of democratic freedoms, allied with what he regarded as working class moral immaturity, would lead to society retrogressing toward a new type of tyranny just as coercive as the power of autocrats – that of the might of the organised majority over the liberty of the individual. In this context, along with working class faith in the power of the state, there resided for Spencer the looming danger to democratic freedoms of socialism (MacRae (ed.), 1969, Spencer, essays entitled The Coming Slavery & From Freedom to Bondage). In this social climate, land nationalization could now also be put on long term hold (Spencer, 1978, Vol.2, Pt.4, Ch.11 & Appendix B).

Spencer viewed continental industrialization as combining state centralization and military aggression (Spencer, 1885a, Vol.1, Pt.2, Ch.11). Competition for control of colonies was a consequence. By the turn of the twentieth century, Britain's colonial exploits in South Africa provided for Spencer further damning evidence of a revival of militancy (In Spencer, 1902, articles entitled Patriotism; Imperialism and Slavery; Re-Barbarization). He argued that militancy was re-establishing its characteristics throughout society, a fact that he believed could be evidenced through the emergence of such varied phenomena as the Salvation Army, school drill, athleticism and Association Football (Spencer, 1902, article entitled Re-Barbarization). As a sign of the times, we can note the emergence of new social theories, such as the social Darwinism of Kidd (1894), now viewing evolution in terms of the survival of the fittest militant societies, followed later in similar vein by the eugenics of such writers as Karl Pearson.

7 | Herbert Spencer
Positivism, Evolution and Progress
Science for Non-intervention

This chapter will look more closely at Spencer's laws of social change and his utilisation of science to argue the normality of gradualism at the advanced social stage and the extension of non-intervention. It will review his law of evolution and view of progress and trace some of the broad consequences to which Spencer argued that this led. More specifically, a number of social policy implications conducive to the dissenting and entrepreneurial middle classes with respect to welfare, education, prison reform and the vote, as well as the status of religion in his system, will be related. Spencer's theory as a reflection of English modernization will be further clarified by reference to his evaluation of French modernization and his opposition to French positivism.

Spencer's positivism
One issue must first be addressed. That is the question of Spencer's 'positivism'. Spencer was highly sensitive to the application of this term to his social theory (Spencer,1904, Vol.2, p.110). To him, 'positivism' referred specifically to Comte's scheme and reference to a theorist as a positivist implied an affinity with the outlook of Comte. The title of Spencer's first major work, Social Statics, could have suggested such an affinity since it corresponded to the term already used by Comte. Spencer had completed Social Statics in 1850. He was apparently only first aware of Comte's works in 1851 through conversations with G.H.Lewes and Georg Eliot. Spencer's defence of his originality, an issue of frequent sensitivity, on this occasion appears to have been well founded. The use of the same term was highly likely to have been fortuitous. It is inconceivable that he would have knowingly allowed his first major work to be entitled by a key conceptual term employed by Comte, a writer toward whom he came to express such profound disagreement. Furthermore, the concept was employed differently by the two men. Social statics, for Comte, referred to the study of the structural and functional integration of society, whereas Spencer used the term in relation to the future social high resting point to which laws of evolution and progress indicated that society would be destined.

Spencer informs us that he did not tackle the French edition of the Cours de Philosophie Positive until 1852 and that due to his poor command of

French he made little progress (Spencer, 1904, Vol.1, p.398). He claimed no detailed knowledge of Comte's work prior to 1854 when he gained access to Harriet Martineau's abridged translation of the Cours (Spencer, 1904, Vol.1, pp.444-445; Duncan, 1908, p.545). Spencer subsequently acknowledged only the indebtedness of clarifying his own position of antagonism to that of Comte (In Spencer, 1878, Vol.3, essay entitled Reasons for Dissenting from the Philosophy of M. Comte).

Despite Spencer's denial on these grounds of his own 'positivism', he held a long standing conviction, traceable back to the early influences of his father, that all phenomena could be understood in terms of natural causation (Spencer, 1904, Vol.1, P.89) and he was preoccupied with establishing a singular science that demonstrated the laws of change. Applied to social phenomena, this approach corresponds with the commonly accepted view of nineteenth century positivism. The author therefore feels justified in applying this term to Spencer's work.

A periodization of Spencer's evolutionism

As a brief overview, the development of Spencer's evolutionism can be periodized as follows:

1. His earliest essays in 1836, which reflected his uncle's religious influence and stern equation of poverty with individual shortcomings (Wiltshire, 1978, pp.19-21), through to Social Statics in 1850, combined a deduction of abstract principles of justice in terms a free enterprise utopia with religious overtones as the basis for ultimate moral rectitude. In Social Statics, whilst retaining reference to a God, Spencer was clearly adopting a deistic position, arguing that human knowledge of the existence of a God as a creator should be founded on rational deduction and observation of the natural world, thus opposing the mysteries of revelation and the hierarchical imposition of church dogma. At this stage in his thinking, Spencer had developed a clear idea of social laws but evolution remained a vague notion.

2. Following Social Statics, naturalistic explanations of social phenomena led Spencer to increasingly question religious explanations of creation. Without yet providing a formula or articulating a mechanism by which change could be explained, in his 1852 essay The Development Hypothesis (Spencer, 1883a) Spencer claimed more evidential support for numerous insensible changes taking place in phenomena over immense lengths of time than for explanation in terms of special creation. This was later followed up by a landmark essay in 1857 (In Spencer, 1883a, Vol.1, essay entitled Progress: Its Law and Cause), in which Spencer first converted naturalistic explanations into a rudimentary formula of cosmic evolution that postulated a

direction of change from simplicity and homogeneity to complexity and heterogeneity in all phenomena. References to supernatural causes of social phenomena were now essentially superfluous, but they did not disappear from his works immediately. For example, in his essay What Knowledge is of Most Worth, first published in July 1859 (In Spencer, 1861), Spencer still made reference to God the creator (p.46, p.50).

3. Between 1857 and the appearance of First Principles in 1862, Spencer worked out the details of his formula of evolution which he claimed provided the highest form of human understanding of change common to all phenomena. It substantiated a position of agnosticism. From First Principles, Spencer became preoccupied with the verification of his formula of evolution in the various volumes of his System of Philosophy (otherwise referred to as the Synthetic Philosophy).

4. Finally, during his last two decades of his writing, Spencer applied his laws of evolution and view of progress to the urgent task of combatting what he believed to be a period of social retrogression. A change of emphasis from immanent (inherent change in an inevitable direction) to non-immanent (change influenced by specific circumstances) evolution (Haines, 1988, Perrin, 1976) was now apparent. This was accompanied by a growing preoccupation with providing a foundation for a relative ethics that was appropriate to the contemporary world (Spencer, 1978), as opposed to an emphasis on absolute ethics which, in Social Statics, he had deduced to provide a compass bearing on social change toward a future utopia.

Atomism and holism in Spencer's works

The question of Spencer's fundamental atomism or holism is of much importance to this text. It is a complex question because the terms have various connotations (Lukes, 1968). Essentially, though, a position of atomism or methodological individualism emphasises that the makeup of elements determines the characteristics of entities made up from aggregates of elements. Holism, by contrast, recognises the emergent quality of entities. Entities have characteristics that are greater than the sum of their element parts and operate according to their own laws. It would be safe to assert that, in a methodological sense, Spencer followed Hobbes and was essentially an atomist. In any phenomena, he claimed, the properties of the elements determine the attributes of the totality (Spencer, 1970, pp.16-18, Spencer, 1880, pp.48-53). For Spencer, the elements of society were individuals whose physical, intellectual and especially moral properties determine the range of workable social institutions and supporting ideas (A position established in Spencer, 1970, and elaborated in Spencer, 1885a, Vol.1, Pt.1, Ch.2-7). However, Spencer also argued that the characteristics of the social environment have a reactive effect on the moral makeup of people, its constituent elements, and that social change can be understood in terms of social laws. There would therefore appear to be a secondary element of holism in Spencer's approach to sociology.

The relationship between social and moral change

For Spencer, social evolution ultimately rested on changes within man, the social unit. Following Lamarck, he argued that these changes were brought about by the inheritance of moral traits that were shaped and only gradually modified by the social environment (Thomson, 1906, Ch.11). Wiltshire (1978, pp.210-212) suggests that this relationship between moral character and social environment led Spencer into an inconsistency of emphasis which needed to be resolved; the question of which was the primary influence?

But was there such an inconsistency and does there need to be a primary influence? For Spencer, the malleability of human nature, through combining inherited moral characteristics with a changing environment, sets a limit to the range of workable social institutions by which order can be established at a specific point in time. Changes in the social environment over time work gradual modifications in human nature (Offer, 1980). Spencer's laws of evolution were to explain the natural direction of structural and functional change and the militant and industrial typology; a measure of the degree of coercive regulation or individual freedom that was an adaptation to the broader environment. The malleability of human nature sets the limit to the pace of orderly social change. Social evolution and progress indicated forward movement in terms increasing social size and sophistication and the breakdown of social constraints on the actions of individuals. Through social change in this direction, man would gradually develop via adaptation to the environment and the inheritance of acquired characteristics the moral qualities of individual responsibility. But if social change were too speedy, he would readily give up individual freedom and responsibility for regulation and protection from the ill consequences of unwise actions. This interpretation Spencer came to relate to the extension of state intervention and a growing climate of collectivism during the 1880s in Britain as evidence of moral immaturity.

Spencer's adherence to free enterprise principles remained throughout his life. He recognised in political economy a sound economic science. However, from his evolutionary perspective, its ideas were a product of the environment of the late eighteenth century. To form an appropriate image of the more evolved future industrial society, these ideas required broadening from an economic into a social model and radicalizing in accordance with man's future moral condition.

Spencer's deism and laws of change

Social Statics (1970) was penned by Spencer during a time in his life and a period in English history which were conducive to a high level of optimism amongst the entrepreneurial middle classes. In this work, he postulated the existence of a beneficent divinity whose only purpose could be for man to be happy. From the principle that man's happiness and fulfilment could only become maximised through the disappearance of external constraints, Spencer deduced a system of absolute moral rectitude as being the perfect realization of God's will on earth. This would be a perfect society of the future – Spencer's delineation of a future utopia.

For Spencer, only by deduction from sound principles and recognition of the existence of natural laws of change at work in society could the analysis of morality move from the uncritical acceptance of tradition and from intuition or opinion to that of a solid and logical foundation (Spencer, 1970, Introduction). Upon this foundation, his far reaching vision portrayed an image of the future that he claimed would astonish many because it was not generalized from the present – a very questionable assertion of course. But it would provide a compass bearing on progress against which social change could be evaluated and by which man could intelligently act to promote God's will on earth. In particular, it would constitute the means to precisely delineate where and where not the state should intervene to act in harmony with the advance of beneficial change. Although Spencer's position was radically non-interventionist, this did not mean that he was averse to the engineering of social change. By arranging social institutions to be incrementally ahead of the prevailing moral condition, evolutionary change could be assisted more effectively than by advanced intellectual arguments as individual behaviour adapted to prevailing institutions.

The ultimate disappearance of external constraints on individual behaviour required social conditions conducive to the realization of the law of equal freedom. This was Spencer's benchmark of absolute justice. Within such a society, each individual would take full responsibility for their own freedom of action whilst ensuring that they did not transgress the equal rights of other individuals. For social harmony to exist in such a social condition, man's internal moral makeup must evolve to a state of enlightened individualism in which it would have become instinctive and automatic for all to know where the boundaries of non-transgressive individual freedom lie, beyond which the encroachment of the freedom of others would result. In the meantime, social and governmental constraints must be in place to the degree to which man's recalcitrant nature must be constrained.

During early civilizations and in medieval times, individuals left free would trample over the rights and freedoms of other individuals. Thus, Spencer argued, coercive and autocratic political control were necessary. Gradual change toward the institutions of democratic government of the mid nineteenth century had been accompanied by a corresponding advance in responsible individualism. For Spencer, the near future held the penultimate stage on the road to utopia in which government intervention could contract to the position of the defence of equal freedom against those who would violate it. Ultimately, even this degree of external regulation would become unnecessary.

In Social Statics, Spencer was optimistic that progressive social change was inherent and immanent. His postulation of natural laws emphasised that change was unilinear. However, his reasoning was teleological in perceiving evidence of God's design and reading purpose into ends. Spencer related the certainty of his social principles and laws of change to his supposedly rationally derived knowledge of God's will (Spencer, 1970, p.66, pp.75-77). Social Statics followed an Enlightenment deist tradition. In so doing, Spencer rejected the revelation, ceremony and superstitions of established religion and based knowledge of God's will on reason (Open University, 1974, Unit 7). In Spencer's hands, deism provided a justification of the Enlightenment formula of 'the greatest happiness to the greatest number'. For Spencer, given human diversity, the individual was the best judge in obtaining his or her happiness. Leaving people free to make their own decisions was thus key to happiness maximization desired by God.

Spencer defined justice as the circumstances in which individuals could freely pursue happiness without transgressing the equal rights of other individuals to do so (Spencer, 1970, Pt.2, Ch.5). To assist social advance, the modern state should restrict its activities to guaranteeing justice. Ideally, the state should have no involvement in regulating the outcome of individual action. 'Allowing' individuals to be accountable for the happiness or misery which naturally followed from their behaviour was regarded as the natural reward for the capable and penalty for the incapable. In the long term, adjustment to this environment would work advantageously through the inheritance of acquired characteristics to improve the human condition toward enlightened individualism – the moral basis for a non-interventionist utopia. Man-made laws, government and state institutions would ultimately be rendered unnecessary since each individual would pursue his or her own interests mindful only of the equal rights of others. The condition of enlightened individualism would thus become the basis for social harmony through non-interventionism, a condition in which, Spencer maintained, God's will would be realized on earth in man's perfect adaptation to the social state. In the meantime, moving to immediate and total non-intervention must be avoided because it would bring anarchy. The government of man by man was therefore a necessary evil proportionate to the evil of man's anti-social but modifiable moral condition (Spencer, 1970, p.14).

Spencer's position in Social Statics can be illustrated via his attack on utilitarianism. Utilitarians shared his happiness maximization outlook and opposition to inefficient traditions. However, he argued, they believed that current social ills should be mitigated through systematic intervention. To Spencer, this was 'expedient' (Spencer, 1970, pp.1-16). It represented an attempted short cut to happiness or the mitigation of misery. Lacking the guidance of (his) long range social laws, utilitarianism was regarded as counterproductive. Through intervention, it undermined the advance of individual responsibility which was the long term moral foundation of happiness maximization. He argued that by assisting the inadequate at cost to the adequate, it was providing a sheltering environment which would in the long run bring retrogression to human nature as it adapted to the social environment. For Spencer, there was no better measure to increase misery and populate the world with fools than to intervene between a fool's folly and its natural consequences (Spencer, 1970, pp.378-381).

At this stage in his thinking, Spencer equated man's intention to increase human happiness through social intervention with an atheistic arrogance that he could do better than to submit to God's laws (Spencer, 1970, p.50, pp.290-295). As well as ordaining laissez faire, this condemnation was a clear reference to the French Revolution and its aftermath and a challenge to the French Enlightenment view of progress through rationally planned social intervention. By contrast, for Spencer, man's highest wisdom would be to know and submit to Divine purpose. Utopia could only be reached by conformity to God's laws of social change which would impose their long term 'beneficent necessity' (Spencer, 1970, p.42). These were laws of progressive non-intervention. Spencer had thus projected his own belief in natural causation into the mind of his God whom he made a far seeing beneficent positivist.

In contrast to the outlook of utilitarianism, Spencer argued that 'we' must brace ourselves for short term miseries to correct 'our' moral imperfections for the long term benefit of mankind (Spencer, 1970, Pt.2, Ch.4). Just who 'we' included had already been made apparent in one of Spencer's earlier letters to The Nonconformist which pre-dated the deism of Social Statics:

> 'though employment be ever so abundant, and society in its most prosperous state, there will still be numerous cases of distress and destitution. Granted; but what follows? In nine cases out of ten that distress results from the transgressions of the individual or his parents: and are we to take away the just punishment of these transgressions? Are we not told that the sins of the wicked shall be visited upon the children of the third and fourth generation?' (Spencer, 1842, Letter 4, p.506).

In such terms, Spencer gives religious sanction to his callous inhumanity toward the sufferings of the poor by citing God's far sighted beneficence. For Spencer, the suffering of individuals invariably indicated individual inadequacy and, in an increasingly meritocratic society, was usually not a result of social injustice. Justice required individuals to face the natural consequences of their behaviour. Progressive non-interventionism would therefore assist improvement in the human condition by allowing the foolish to face the full consequences of their folly, and presumably fall by the wayside, and the wise and able to benefit from their talents. In support of free enterprise and the notion of the self-made-man, Spencer attacked the privileges of the aristocracy and what he saw as their misguided paternalism toward the poor. Care had also to be taken against unwise humanitarian intervention which could hold greater appeal with the advance of moral sensibilities. On the other hand, Spencer avoided analysis of the comparative life chances of the middle classes and the poor through his view of their respective just deserts based on the inheritance of acquired characteristics. Spencer retained this position when he later withdrew the authority of God from his analysis.

Social policy guidance on the issue of welfare was clear. Welfare should be based on desert and not need (Offer, 1983, discusses the implications of this view). In modern industrial societies, the provision of state charity was regarded by Spencer as retrogressive (Spencer, 1970, Ch.25) because it undermined the beneficial link between the assumed improvidence of the majority of the poor and its natural consequence of suffering. Operating at the macro level, state welfare provision would impose on the provident a financial penalty to make possible the impersonal distribution of charity to the needy through an inefficient mechanism. The needy improvident would became accustomed to this inefficient means of public assistance. Consequently, as well as assisting a retrogression in human nature, the state mechanism of redistribution took more from the total pool of happiness than it gave. For Spencer, the state should only guarantee justice – the non-transgression of individual freedoms. Personal philanthropy (Spencer, 1978, Vol.2, Pt.6, Ch.7) was the only viable alternative to state charity. Enlightened individuals should be discerningly beneficent toward the poor. They would be well placed to distinguish the unfortunate poor deserving their assistance from the improvident who did not. In cases where charity was deserved, the altruism of the provider and the recipient's gratitude would be moral qualities enhanced in the assistance directly given. State intervention to assist the poor would undermine the development of these moral qualities. Its advocacy was based on ignorance of social laws. Enlightened social policy therefore required the improvident to be left to suffer for the benefit of posterity.

Spencer's early works were penned during the period of his involvement in radical middle class politics. In view of the above quotation and comments, it would seem ironic that he acted as a local representative of the Complete Suffrage Union. But the solution to this irony lies in another of his early letters on The Proper Sphere of Government (Spencer, 1842, Letter 10, p.827). Spencer was at this time optimistic that government intervention was destined to decline. He was therefore happy for the vote to be extended to the working class and women because it would represent a declining source of political power. He later, in Social Statics, supported the extension of the franchise on the basis of the holistic notion that the moral condition is always relatively uniform throughout society (Spencer, 1970, pp.222-226). The working class and women were therefore as entitled to the vote as anyone else.

Spencer's methodological atomism led him to maintain that all individuals should profess and act out their sincerely held beliefs. Only by such means could the outcome act as a social barometer to indicate which social institutions would be best adapted to the aggregate condition of individuals as social elements. This view implied a democratic assumption of the equality of social input between individuals. In Social Statics, Spencer asserted that

'Not as adventitious, therefore, will the wise man regard the faith that is in him – not as something which may be slighted, and made subordinate to calculations of policy; but as the supreme authority to which all his actions should bend. The highest truth conceivable by him he will fearlessly utter; and will endeavour to get embodied in fact his purist idealisms: knowing that, let what may come of it, he is thus playing his appointed part in the world – knowing that if he can get done the thing he aims at – well: if not – well also; though not so well' (Spencer, 1970, p.475).

The same point was expressed over a decade later by Spencer in First Principles (Spencer, 1946, pp.101-102). This lesson was happily drawn when Spencer was optimistic that social change was on the side of the entrepreneurial middle classes.

Toward a theory of evolution

Scientific advances in the first half of the nineteenth century were challenging traditional religious assumptions and pointing toward evolutionism (Thomson, 1906, Ch.10). As well as Lamarck's theory relating the diversity of life to the inherited effect of environmental changes, Lyell's geological findings dated the earth at millions of years. Evidence of primitive man had also been uncovered. Laplace's Nebular Hypothesis envisaged a process of growing heterogeneity in the solar system from a nebulous state through cooling gasses, and Von Baer had demonstrated that the growth of organisms involved change from relative uniformity to a relatively multiform structure. Spencer was aware of these and other scientific developments (Spencer, 1904, Vol.1, p.176 & p.174; Spencer, 1946, p.371). By 1852, their influence was evident in his essay The Development Hypothesis (Spencer, 1883a, Vol.1). This essay opposed to the view of supernatural creation one which Spencer argued provided superior evidential support; that of the modifying effect of natural influences working over great periods of time a vast number of insensible changes on all phenomena. But Spencer still needed to piece together his scientific insights and recognize a common thread to hit on his theory of cosmic evolution. He would achieve this in reviewing in his broad range of essays.

The impact of science did not just fall on a narrow intellectual elite. The Victorian middle classes were avid readers of journals and intrigued by scientific demonstrations and new gadgetry. The broader public witnessed the applications of scientific progress all around them. To the extent that science was challenging traditional religious dogma as a basis of morality, it gave rise to both the need and the means for a cosmic scientific theory as a secular basis for moral guidance. As a dissenter who was becoming an agnostic, Spencer, unlike Darwin who, as an Anglican with aristocratic connections, had for over twenty years confined his ideas on evolution to his secret notebooks (Desmond and Moore, 1991), held little reluctance to publish work that might upset the religious establishment. The breakthrough came in his 1857 essay Progress: Its Law and Cause (In Spencer, 1883a). In this essay, Spencer argued that the ultimate causes of all phenomena were unknown and unknowable to human intelligence. The scientifically informed position on questions of religion was therefore one of agnosticism. What could be known was the changes taking place in observable phenomena. Whilst acknowledging the thinness of verifying evidence in a number of areas, Spencer defined evolutionary change as that from nebulous simple and uniform structures to that of clearly crystallised complex and multiform structures. This he illustrated by tracing changes in art, language and society.

Unfortunately, wedded to the Lamarckian view of the inheritance of acquired characteristics, Spencer was not able to quite make the insightful leap that Darwin did. For Darwin, the Lamarckian view of inheritance did not provide the dynamic necessary to explain the extent of species modification. Darwin's great insight was that in the struggle for existence, species variation, in relation to environment, provided evolutionary benefit through eliminating unfavourable changes and enhancing the survival procreation and inheritance potential associated with favourable variation (Roark, 2004, pp.7-12).

Spencer's materialist theory of evolution

Spencer's theory of evolution reached fruition in his formula for cosmic evolution expounded in First Principles, published in 1862. All phenomena were now explained in materialist terms in the philosophical sense of matter and motion, a position that had been adopted by a number of French Enlightenment thinkers (Open University, 1974, Unit 7).

In First Principles, Spencer represented cosmic evolution as the highest form of scientific knowledge because, he argued, it expressed change in all phenomena according to a single law. Through its cosmic applicability, this law required the analysis of all change to be expressed in the form of mechanical categories. Cosmic evolution portrayed change in all phenomena in terms of space, time, matter, motion and force (Spencer, 1946, Pt.2, Ch.3), with evolutionary change involving a process of increasing differentiation and integration. Applied to all organic entities, evolutionary changes exhibited increasingly complex structures and specialized functions of more clearly discernible parts operating with increasing precision, integration and co-ordination within the organic whole. In its social application, Spencer claimed for evolution an immunity from bias because it rested on laws of impersonal forces which operated throughout nature and the universe. These laws for Spencer pointed toward an efficient, harmonious, non-interventionist industrial society as the most highly evolved social condition.

Spencer's masterpiece on social evolution was his Principles of Sociology. In focussing on particular societies, he gave greater recognition to change in the form of adaptation to local circumstances which may retard or enhance the process. Consequently, change in particular societies became viewed less as intrinsic or immanent. He also introduced the militant and industrial social typology and scale of change (Spencer, 1885a, Vol.1, Pt.2, Ch.10). The use of two scales of change has caused some confusion for which Spencer has been largely responsible through his vague use of terminology. The confusion is in Spencer's reference to the processes of both evolution and progress, with for example Rumney (1966, p.271) strangely asserting that for Spencer 'progress is automatic and inherent in the cosmos and in every part of it'. Rumney was surely referring to evolution instead.

Spencer intertwined evolution with progress by using two scales of change. When he referred to change toward the industrial social type, he invariably made reference to the process of evolution. However, movement away from this type was usually referred to as 'retrogression'. But to retrogress is the opposite to progress, not evolution. When Spencer used the term retrogression, he invariably referred to reversion toward militant type social characteristics. The militant and industrial scale was certainly used by Spencer a scale of progress and held a strong evaluative aspect. Social evolution referred more formally to change of structure and function accompanied by social growth and compounding. But growth and compounding were intimately related to the use of force during the period of militancy. Spencer in fact interrelated social evolution and social progress and gave them a tendency toward a common outcome in the industrial society, but progress was more vulnerable to reversal.

The future pure industrial society for Spencer was a free enterprise capitalist society of possessive individualism and entrepreneurialism. Spencer remained loyal to this model even when later in the nineteenth century the nature of business organisations was changing with the spread of joint stock companies. The possessive individualism model stood opposed to the growth of large organizational structures, the separation of ownership from control and the concentration of power in oligarchical structures dominated by directors and excessive employer power over employees. Instead, the perfect society would comprise economically motivated self-supporting individuals working in a self-employed capacity, within small private businesses or worker co-operatives and rewarded according to their efforts and abilities within a free market system. The state would contract to its minimal negative interventionist role as guarantor of justice between enlightened individuals and nations would engage peacefully in free trade.

Progress to the industrial society referred to changes in the organization of society from centralization to extreme decentralization. Even with the advance of industry, these changes would be influenced by the nature of external relations with other societies. Relations could be warlike of peaceful. Relationships of aggression would necessitate the internal regulation of all spheres of life and the subordination of the individual to the cause of social survival or expansion in combatant nations. This was the militant type. For characteristics of the industrial type to advance, peaceful co-existence would be necessary to facilitate free trade between societies and deregulation within.

Evolution tended toward the same goal. Likewise to evolutionary levels within organisms, primitive societies comprised a relatively homogenous mass whilst highly evolved societies would become heterogeneous systems (Spencer, 1946, Pt.2, Ch.14-17). Primitive societies comprised small aggregates of like members (Spencer, 1885a, Vol.1, pp.459-460). As hunters or agriculturalists, they used the simplest of implements and lived from hand to mouth. Comprising little hierarchy, division of labour, or economic integration, the aggregate was able to divide up with minimal damage to the social organism. Correspondingly, according to Spencer, impulsiveness and improvidence characterised man's primitive moral nature (Spencer, 1885a, Vol.1, Pt.1, Ch.6).

Societies in evolution exhibited growth in population and area occupied by the process of natural growth and levels of compounding, particularly through conquest. The latter constituted the evolutionary process of survival of the fittest within an environment of antagonism between societies. The relationship between societies inevitably links evolution with progress. Efficient defensive or offensive action required the emergence of hierarchy, a regulative centre, and an extension of the division of labour from a primitive condition of social homogeneity. The emergence of militant societies from such primitive social aggregates was therefore structurally and functionally evolutionary. For Spencer, it also moulded a recalcitrant human nature to social discipline as an imperative for social survival.

Individual freedom to pursue an appropriate specialized occupation was a consequence of structural and functional changes accompanying the growth of the social organism. Through growth, population pressure necessitated the greater productive efficiency made possible by the extension of the division of labour, technological advance (Spencer, 1946, pp.289-290) and the exchange relations of a more free market. This would allow further population growth (Spencer, 1946, pp.408-409). As the conditions of the industrial society approached, factors facilitating population stability would come into play. Spencer maintained that higher survival rates of progeny and lower reproduction rates were characteristic of highly evolved species (the opposite applying to lower evolutionary levels). At man's most civilised state, the increased psychic demands accompanying competitive individualism would lead to declining fertility rates. This would be compatible with a higher survival rate of offspring and enable more caring relationships to exist between parents and children. Despite his previously noted hard strictures toward the poor, this evolutionary insight enabled Spencer to be more optimistic than Malthus on the general population question.

It is vital to appreciate that Spencer's militant and industrial typology was a social typology. It referred to the nature of social organization which was shaped by inter-societal relationships rather than simply the degree of industrial development (Spencer, 1885b, Vol.2, Pt.5, pp.603-604). Rumney's (1966) criticism that the types were not mutually exclusive because industrial societies could also be warlike therefore misses the point. However, this emphasis on the social in the use of his types has led Spencer to another awkward classificatory matter. Peaceable societies which were primitive in his evolutionary terms and which had developed very little industry or industriousness could nevertheless be classified as 'industrial' (Spencer, 1885b, Vol.2, Pt.5, p616). Conditions of peace between social groups reinforce individual freedom and moral amity which for Spencer were characteristic of the future industrial type. There is therefore just detectable in Spencer's works a hint of a three stage historical model (like Marx, but with different types) of primitive 'industrial', militant, and emerging modern industrial types.

We have already seen that evolution and progress did not therefore necessarily advance simultaneously. It can now be added that from peaceful primitive 'industrial' societies, social compounding and the associated growth of a regulative apparatus indicated evolution to a more complex social structure. But this also represented, in a sense, retrogression from an early version of the 'industrial' to the militant type.

Nevertheless, since the development of industrial technique enhanced the prospect of supplementing wealth through peaceful co-existence, it linked evolution and progress in the direction of the industrial society. The battle for survival between militant societies could be replaced by an external relationship of beneficial competition through free trade and internally by free competition between enlightened individuals. However, an environment of uncertain relations between societies always kept open the possibility of retrogression toward militancy. Despite the optimism of Spencer's earlier works, his theory did not attempt to guarantee that industrialization would not be used for military purposes. Indeed, during the latter part of the nineteenth century, he became increasingly preoccupied with the re-emergence of militancy in England, much of the blame for which he placed on what he saw as a militant form of industrialization followed by such continental powers as France and Germany (Spencer, 1885a, Vol.1, Pt.2, Ch.11).

The militant society was a social environment that corresponded to man's callous moral nature. Social cohesion required regimentation and repressive institutions. Spencer argued that social change during this phase would be irregular, violent and dramatic in the form of revolution, anarchy and reaction. The advance of the industrial type represented a withering away of repressive institutions accompanied by the gradual progress of enlightened individualism. This social type would increasingly represent a responsive and self-adjusting social organism. By contrast to the militant society, this more plastic social form would advance peaceably and gradually through a process of continuous incremental adjustments (Spencer, 1946, pp.460-461). By this analysis and in terms of this comparison, Spencer argued that by the 1850s England had reached a stage of relative maturity compared to more militant France.

Spencer's use of the biological analogy

Spencer attempted to substantiate his view of free enterprise capitalism as a highly evolved social organism through analogy with highly evolved biological organisms (In Spencer, 1883a, Vol.1, essay entitled The Social Organism; Spencer, 1885a, Vol.1, Pt.2). For Spencer, evolutionary similarities included tendencies toward greater mass from small origins, increasing complexity of structure and function, and mutual interdependence of increasingly specialized parts. As in highly evolved biological organisms, so in highly evolved social organisms, the consequences for the whole of damage to the parts would be especially far reaching. For example, a strike by a section of workers would have detrimental consequences for the whole social organism.

In both the individual and social organism, growth is dependent of functional efficiency in providing an excess of nutrient. In the case of society, growth is dependent on profit which for Spencer is analogous to an excess of nutrition over waste in the individual organism. The social nutrient is commodities, which, with the evolution of the social organism, become increasingly abundant and varied. As, in highly evolved biological organisms, there is development of sophisticated blood and nervous systems, so in highly evolved societies the circulation of commodities is accompanied by a sophisticated system of transport and communications. Carrying the analogy to a level of quite literal comparison, Spencer pointed to railway lines with telegraph systems running alongside as analogous to arteries and nerves respectively in bodily systems (In Spencer, 1883a, Vol.1, essay entitled The Social Organism). In each case, the higher organism has the higher rate of metabolism.

But could Spencer's analogy between biological organisms and society fully sustain the model of a highly evolved free enterprise society? T.H. Huxley thought not. He pointed to fundamental contradictions in the inferences drawn by Spencer (In Huxley, 1893, Ch6, essay entitled Administrative Nihilism; Duncan 1908, p.150; Wiltshire, 1978, pp.183-185) which Spencer struggled to counter (In Spencer, 1878, Vol.3, essay entitled Specialized Administration). Huxley argued that if the withering away of the state regulatory apparatus represented the high point of social evolution, it would indicate a corresponding high point in biological organisms having no nervous or intelligent directing centre. This was clearly very far from the case. More recently, Andreski (1972, pp.28-29) has posed the contradiction the other way round. He has pointed out that since in biological organisms represented by Spencer's scheme the most highly evolved have the most sophisticated directive centres, we would expect by analogy the most evolved societies to be regulated by a highly sophisticated state apparatus. The fact that Spencer also drew distinctions between the social and the biological organism (for example, the dispersal of sentient life throughout and the physical separation of elements in the social organism which are not evident in the biological organism) is little defence on such a fundamental matter since the law of evolution was meant to be a singular law of parallel not opposite changes. When for Spencer the question of consistency between his social preferences and the implications of his science was raised, the social preferences prevailed and scientific credibility was stretched.

The knowable, the unknowable and religion
Spencer placed his evolutionism as the highest generalization knowable of the process of law like change common to all phenomena. As such, it realized his goal of philosophical generalization and scientific unity (Spencer, 1946, Pt.2, Ch.1). He maintained that whilst the mechanistic understanding that it made available represented the limits of human knowledge, the categories employed were only symbolic conceptions of an underlying reality which would remain for ever inscrutable due to the limited intellectual capacity of man (Spencer, 1946, Pt.1, Ch.4). To Spencer, there existed scientific knowledge of phenomena through mechanical laws and causal sequences. First causes and the unconditioned represented the unknowable. There was nothing intelligible in between. The limits to our scientific understanding of any phenomena resided in tracing its changes according to mechanically expressed evolutionary laws from its earliest measurable appearance to its disappearance (Spencer, 1946, p.246). The creation of something from nothing was both impossible to conceive or prove. It was for ever beyond the province of science but

for some belief in supernatural creation would remain a matter of faith (Spencer, 1946, Pt.1, Ch.4). For Spencer, religious faith had its basis in mans' consciousness but also incomprehension of an inscrutable and unconditioned realm which however much science should advance would remain for ever beyond the scope of human knowledge (Spencer, 1946, Pt.1, Ch.4, & p.81). Whilst its representations change, a sense of mystery and wonder that lies at the heart of religious consciousness would probably therefore never disappear (Spencer, 1946, p.93).

The enlightened scientific attitude toward religion should therefore be one of agnosticism, not an atheistic scientific intolerance (Spencer, 1946, pp.99-101). Religion and evolutionism did not have to be in sharp conflict, since Spencer's evolutionism left the question of first causes open. This was an open door through which he felt that theologians could tolerate his evolutionism. Yet, in some cases, Spencer found the reaction of theologians toward evolution to exhibit 'the tenacious vitality of superstitions' (In Spencer, 1883a, Vol.1, essay entitled The Development Hypothesis). They required from evolutionism, and were supplied with, greater evidential support than could be found in favour of supernatural creation, but adhered to the latter as a matter of faith. Consequently, Spencer had to defend his evolutionism from the theological hostility of such writers as Mr. Martineau (In Spencer, 1878, Vol.3, essay entitled Mr. Martineau on Evolution), Lord Salisbury (In Spencer, 1901, Vol.1, essay entitled Lord Salisbury on Evolution) and Professor Tait (In Spencer, 1897, article entitled Professor Tait on the Formula of Evolution). With the development of science and through moral evolution, Spencer argued that religious conceptions would change from an awareness of the personal supernatural to that of an impersonal force (Spencer, 1946, Pt.1, Ch.5; Spencer, 1885c, Vol.3, Pt.6, Ch.16). When this stage is reached, the behaviour of enlightened individuals would not have to be checked by fear of retribution from a personal God any more than by a despot or a repressive state.

With the formula of evolution to explain social change, the will of a personal God was no longer necessary as the source of natural laws in Spencer's scheme. For God Spencer substituted the unknowable which was pushed into the background of the formula of evolution which explained the knowable in mechanical terms and causal processes.

By contrast, Comte's religion of humanity had proposed that the known, the best of humanity, should be the object of worship in the positivist society. In his exchange with the supporter of Comte, Frederic Harrison, Spencer argued that even the noblest of humanity was not worthy of worship. Such personification represented a retrogressive religion and the associated ritual and ceremony were characteristics of militancy.

Additionally, he argued that the known could not be an appropriate object of awe which could only relate to an ongoing sense of mystery (Spencer, 1884). For Spencer, evolution and progress were essentially bi-polar scales of social change. The advance of enlightenment could be assisted by the identification of rituals and ceremonies as unwanted survivals from medievalism to be rooted out – a view which for Spencer, like Tylor, reflected a modernist and puritanical background. There was no search for a future version of the past which came to characterize Comte's three stage model.

Spencer's view of science

How did Spencer define science? Spencer held a pragmatic theory of knowledge (Peel, 1971, pp.117-118). For him there was no fundamental separation between scientific knowledge and ordinary knowledge (In Spencer, 1883a, Vol.1, essay entitled The Genesis of Science & in Spencer, 1897, article entitled An Element in Method). Both enabled predictions to be based on a systematization of knowledge. Comparing everyday knowledge with scientific knowledge was akin to comparing undeveloped science with developed science. The distinction was not in the nature of the thinking or the certainty of prediction, but in the complexity of inferences and their remoteness from direct perception. Undeveloped science comprised sensations largely unaided by measuring devices and allowed largely qualitative prevision derived from knowledge of only simple laws. The hallmark of developed science was that the senses were aided by increasingly sophisticated measuring devices which allowed for quantitative prevision of the precise magnitude of effects. More complex laws could become recognized and accurate prediction and measurement allowed deductions to be made which would not be possible through the direct senses. With its advance, science became a more systematic and conscious pursuit (In Spencer, 1897, article entitled An Element in Method).

How did he characterise the evolution of science? Spencer denied the validity of Comte's law of the three stages and his hierarchy of the sciences (In Spencer, 1883a, Vol.1, essay entitled The Genesis of Science & in Spencer, 1878, Vol.3, essay entitled Reasons for Dissenting from the Philosophy of M. Comte). He also disputed the view that systems of ideas determine the social condition and that the intellect regulates behaviour (as emphasised in Comte's early works) (In Spencer, 1878, Vol.3, essay entitled Reasons for Dissenting from the Philosophy of M. Comte). There was no fixed subject hierarchical sequence through which knowledge passed from pre-scientific to scientific. The advance of science from undeveloped to developed implied for Spencer a greater continuity of thinking and took place across a broad front of collateral influences (In Spencer, 1878, Vol.3, essay entitled Reasons for Dissenting from the Philosophy of M. Comte). Whilst it was agreed that social phenomena were the most complex, Spencer argued that the advance of science was based on many other factors (such as perceived practical importance) than the simplicity and generality of the subject matter that were the determining factors for Comte (In Spencer, 1878, Vol.3, essay entitled Reasons for Dissenting from the Philosophy of M. Comte).

In Spencer's scheme of universal evolution, increasing specialization, integration and co-ordination were as much a characteristic of the realm of ideas as of the structure of the social organism. Discoveries made in more sharply specialized areas of knowledge would both increasingly rely on and feed into other specialized areas so that the overall consensus of knowledge increased as science advanced across a broad front (In Spencer, 1883a, Vol.1, essay entitled The Genesis of Science, pp. 184-189). The ultimate synthesis of specializations lay in the single law of evolution itself, the acceptance of which was itself based on an advanced social and moral condition. Like Comte, Spencer found justification of his own scheme as the highest achievement within itself.

Science and social policy

The contrast in Comte's and Spencer's views on the nature and development of science, society and the individual held important implications for their model systems of education. Both theorists were recapitulationists; they saw the development of the individual to mirror the development of humanity. For Comte, a sound education thus had to follow sequentially his hierarchy of the sciences, since the mastery of each subject presupposed a foundation in those lower in the hierarchy. To Spencer, this was imposing a mistaken hierarchy into the educational process (In Spencer, 1883a, Vol.1, essay entitled The Genesis of Science, pp. 192-193). It was rigid, dogmatic and authoritarian and reflected the French tradition of state centralization which indicated a more militant condition than prevailed in England.

By contrast, Spencer's system supported his dissenting stance of hostility toward all state education (Spencer, 1970, Ch.26). He emphasised the importance of direct parental responsibility (Spencer, 1970, pp.352-355) and a more liberal and naturalistic education such as his own. Parents should acquire a general knowledge of the evolution of the individual (In Spencer, 1861, essay entitled Intellectual Education). Parental upbringing of their children could then encourage the natural unfolding of their qualities. Since man was surrounded by a world of constraining natural laws, which included those operative in the social sphere, the most useful educational guidance would be to help children understand and face the natural consequences of their actions (In Spencer, 1861, essay entitled Moral Education). This required a gradual transition from protective guidance of the child as an appropriate ethics of family life, to the discipline of social ethics through eventual full exposure of the mature individual to the natural consequences of their behaviour. This reasoning was consistent with Spencer's broader scheme. A rigid pedagogic education could not benefit the individual or assist social evolution because evolution was determined not by the intellectual condition but by the moral condition and the moral condition could only evolve through individuals learning from experience with minimal state intervention to bail them out (In Spencer, 1883b, Vol.2, essay entitled Over-Legislation).

A similar logic underpinned policy guidance in the area of prison reform (In Spencer, 1883b, Vol.2, essay entitled Prison Ethics). For Spencer, a compass bearing of absolute morality appropriate to the fully evolved industrial society, tempered by the expediency of the present stage of evolution, would provide the best guidance for prison reform. The state of average popular character will ultimately determine both the necessary degree of repressive government and severity of penalties against the criminal. Given the predatory moral condition that was characteristic of the militant environment, penalties against perpetrators needed to be vengeful, severe and immediate, providing, along with political despotism, the only alternative to the greater suffering of social anarchy. By contrast, the amelioration of the general moral condition toward enlightened individualism associated with the industrial society heightens the sensitivity of individuals to the consequences of their actions on others. The extent of this advance should establish the degree to which a less repressive political environment and vengeful penal system are possible in which the primary aim should be to provide restitution to victims. In essence, prison should be a microcosm environment for the reshaping of the defective morality of the offender through establishing the conditions that link behaviour to its natural and just consequences which the criminal tried to circumvent. For Spencer, this would be a rigorous regime of self-maintenance.

Social science and non-intervention in the industrial society

Spencer argued that social science could itself only reach maturity in the industrial society. This is because feelings, sympathies and the moral condition largely determine acceptable modes of thinking. Under militancy, the moral condition necessary for social survival was not conducive to the advance of social science. The ethos of 'might is right' and the worship of power would introduce patriotic, religious, class and political bias, which would be functional for that stage of society, into the analysis of social phenomena (Spencer, 1880). By contrast, peace and enlightened individualism associated with the fully evolved industrial type would allow a balanced judgement of social phenomena along with enhanced moral sensitivity to the far reaching effects of our actions on others.

Growing social scientific knowledge would, further, indicate the folly of interventionism simultaneous to its lesser requirement. This was the chief enlightening aim of Spencer's sociology. Advances in social scientific knowledge were demonstrating that the consequences of state intervention were so detailed and far reaching that they would extend incalculably beyond their original design with an excess of unanticipated and counterproductive consequences (In Spencer, 1883b, Vol.2, essay entitled Over-Legislation, p.63; Spencer, 1970, pp.8-12). This would be especially so in a highly sophisticated, integrated and evolved social organism of the industrial type. Spencer's grouse was that currently, for politicians, often of classical education and underdeveloped scientific outlook (features of the militant type), the answers to social problems were deceptively simple and only some of the short term consequences of intervention would be anticipated. They held a woefully inadequate conception of the highly complex social phenomena to which they applied their legislation. But, argued Spencer, no individual or controlling centre would be able to calculate all of the far reaching outcomes of its interventions. Only through the wisdom acquired by freely co-operating individuals attempting to maximize their happiness in a self-adjusting system could monumental mistakes through state intervention be avoided. Enlightenment in social science would lead to enhanced awareness of our ignorance in social matters. Political humility would thus progress with social scientific knowledge in the complex industrial society.

Spencer even extended the principle of non-intervention to medical science in dealing with the complex biological organism (Spencer, 1902, article entitled Vaccination). To the extent that vaccination brought effective defence against a specific disease, Spencer maintained that it must rearrange the body's defensive system with unknown consequences. Evidence suggested, Spencer claimed, that the control of one disease through vaccination had been related to epidemics of others. The biological and social analogy offered a convenient convergence in the conclusion that the state should therefore not tamper!

There would appear to be a neat fit to Spencer's view of social science and social non-intervention. However, even accepting his evolutionism, one vital question remained unasked. How did the rate of evolution of social scientific knowledge compare to that of the evolving complexity of social phenomena itself? Only if it were slower could non-interventionism be placed on a sound foundation. As Spencer left it, his foundation remained his long standing conviction in non-interventionism.

8 | Herbert Spencer
A Rear Guard Defence of
Non-Interventionism

The purpose of this chapter will be to look at Spencer's theory of evolution and progress in the context of his response to the changing social circumstances of the late nineteenth century. In particular, scrutiny will be made of the extent to which the application of his theoretical position remained consistent in response to social changes which he regarded as retrogressive. Spencer retained his radical anti-state position during a period of growing state interventionism. To what extent did his social policy recommendations change? Is a growing conservatism detectable in Spencer's position? Did any changes derive from the consistent application of fixed principles to changed circumstances, or did his social preferences come to override the consistent application of his scientific principles? These questions must be put in the context of the rise of working class collectivism, feminism, new liberalism, and colonialism of the latter decades of the nineteenth century.

Spencer's evolutionism and view of progress offered a signpost for the direction of social advance with the warning that the journey would be a long, slow and painful one. Evolution and progress pointed to the gradual extension and ultimately absolute achievement of non-intervention. However, the growing power of the working class and their preference for state intervention and collective action to individualism was regarded by Spencer as retrogressive. One form that working class power took was through trade unionism. By the 1880s, Spencer argued that growing union organization and activity amongst unskilled workers was subverting the workings of a free enterprise economy. To Spencer, the opposition of the might of organized collectivities to individual freedom of contract and the tendency of collective majorities to trample over the rights of individuals represented the re-emergence of militancy (In MacRae (ed.) 1969, essay entitled From Freedom to Bondage).

Social engineering now required defensive measures to be put in place to restrict such retrogressive tendencies. As early as 1860, in his essay Parliamentary Reform: The Dangers and the Safeguards (Spencer, 1883b, Vol.2), Spencer came to urge caution in the extension of the vote to the working class. He feared that they retained a false and archaic view of the potency of the state. This view he regarded as a survival of a more primitive mentality (See Ch.6). If the vote were to be extended, the illusion that the state can create something from nothing had first to be dispelled to guard against an outcome of retrogression toward socialism. This could not be accomplished by appeal to the intellect or the extension of education since for Spencer the intellect is subservient to feelings and the prevailing moral condition. It had to be related to practical interest through the manipulation of institutional arrangements. The safeguard that Spencer advocated was the limitation of the vote to those who contributed to state expenditure – the taxpayers. Fearful of the expansion of the state, Spencer abandoned his earlier advocacy of complete suffrage. He instead proposed the engineering of a restriction of the sphere of government by skewing the political influence deriving from the vote in favour of the middle classes and the 'responsible' sections of the working class. Such a restricted electorate would largely comprise those who would want to limit the level taxation that they pay, much of which would be used as expenditure through which others as non-contributors would be the main beneficiaries. It would lock out from electoral influence those who tended to reatin a view of the magical potency of the state, a view associated with receiving benefits provided by the state that were not paid for.

For Spencer, the lower status occupied by women in militant societies was a barrier to refined affections. This barrier could only recede with the decline of barbarism. Yet he also came to view the outlook of women as retrogressive and became opposed to extending their political influence in contemporary society. Spencer asserted that, in relation to men, women have a lesser capacity for abstract reasoning that could lead to a recognition of his sense of justice. They retained an awe for authority and held less respect for individual freedoms. Women preferred the protective ethics of the family to the competitive ethics of society. Their influence on the political landscape would therefore inappropriately, according to Spencer, tend to fall in favour of state protection. Since the opposing family and social ethics must be kept within their separate bounds, the influence of women should remain a domestic one.

When applied to the working class and women, Spencer no longer argued, as he had in Social Statics, from the egalitarian position that the moral condition was relatively uniform throughout society. He also seemed to forget his previous assertion that social institutions will naturally reflect the overall moral state. Perhaps this was because the best test of the moral state would be through the universal suffrage which Spencer, during a time of optimism in the advance of entrepreneurial individualism had once advocated, along with the (unlikely) implication that if it led to interventionism, then so be it.

Likewise, his earlier assertions that all individuals should openly argue their honestly held convictions and attempt to influence society accordingly for the overall outcome of opinion to be accurately registered (See Ch.7) had been replaced by 1873 with the more cautious advice that

'the man of higher type must be content with greatly moderated expectations, while he perseveres with undiminished efforts. He has to see how comparatively little can be done, and yet find it worth while to do that little; so uniting philanthropic energy with philosophic calm' (Spencer, 1880, p.398).

In Social Statics, Spencer had opposed the absolute property rights of the aristocracy. Their inherited landed wealth represented idle wealth as opposed to the active wealth created by the industrious middle classes. At this point in time he had adopted a deistic theological position that land was God's bequest to mankind. The pattern of ownership which had emerged was the outcome of earlier appropriation by force under social conditions of militancy. It defied the law of equal freedom of access to land which was appropriate to the industrial society. Land should therefore ultimately be returned to the community (Spencer, 1970, Ch.9).

When, in the later climate of growing socialist opinion, the land reformer Henry George, in his work Progress and Poverty, drew attention to Spencer's earlier deduced principles, Spencer hedged the possibility of their application with various qualifications. Earlier militant transgressions in the acquisition of land remained acknowledged. However, he argued that it was unlikely that the present landowners and landless were respectively the direct descendants of the original dispossessors and dispossessed respectively. History clouded our knowledge of the transfer of property. Dispossession of the present owners would therefore be inequitable. Even dispossession with compensation would be prohibitive if allowance were to be made for the value of land improvements over the generations from virgin to its present state. And wouldn't state administration in attempting to do so, he argued, be highly inefficient? Spencer now argued the pragmatism of adopting a position of relative ethics as opposed to his previous stance of absolute ethics by recognizing existing arrangements as acceptable for the present stage of progress. Henry George took up these and other issues to indicate Spencer's retraction from the practical implications of his earlier principles (George, 1893). The Spencer of Social Statics that was published in 1850 (a much later publication of the text had the offending chapter on land nationalization omitted) and who was a radical opponent of the aristocracy and a critic of utilitarianism as an expediency theory had drawn closer to the establishment and directed his radical fire power against the working class.

Spencer remained strongly anti-state interventionist in matters of welfare. For him, social evolution relied on allowing individual superiority or inferiority to obtain their natural rewards. We have seen (Ch.7) that Spencer largely ignored the effect of differing life chances in his view of individual superiority because of the emphasis that he placed on the inheritance of acquired traits. He argued that through individual competition and responsibility, the superior amongst the working class would be self-motivated toward success. Whilst allowances can be made for instances of poverty through misfortune, where individual beneficence toward others can be justified, Spencer's essential position was that living in poverty in a society viewed as providing opportunity for all was in the vast majority of cases proof of individual moral inferiority, as in the case of the idle poor who refused to work, and should not be tampered with by state support for them. In this analysis, Spencer's biology overwhelmed his sociology. The inheritance of poverty could be seen in terms of the inheritance of inferior moral traits. Spencer was not prepared to recognize the environmental impact of misfortune as being the systematic and potentially overwhelming outcome of the inheritance of restricted life chances, related to the vastly unequal distribution of private wealth and income.

On this point, the Italian Marxist Ferri (1905) took issue with Spencer. He argued that in supporting free enterprise capitalism, Spencer's evolutionism provided a positive analysis of social change up to that point in time, with capitalism offering improved opportunity for the fit and able to flourish compared to the institutions of feudalism. But his evolutionism had stopped short of its logical conclusion. Evolution based truly on survival of the fittest required a social system that placed competition on an equal footing. For Ferri, this could only be possible through future social evolution to a new social system whereby common ownership of the means of production replaced a system in which ownership of such resources and the advantages that they bestow could be acquired through the inheritance of private property. Only the transition from capitalism to communism would maximize the individual's liberty to fully demonstrate and benefit from their personal aptitudes.

Fabian socialists in England opposed Marxist revolutionary socialism as utopian (Webb, S. et al, 1962, Preface). Instead, they emphasised the gradualist approach of evolution toward a socialist society. This entailed the progressive extension of those changes that Spencer attacked as retrogressive, most pointedly in his Man Versus the State essays (MacRae (ed.), 1969) – municipalisation, publicly regulated and owned joint stock companies and labour legislation to regulate work hours and minimum wages. Full extension of the franchise was advocated as was the provision of welfare for those unable to work and the imposition of progressive taxation (In Webb, S. et al, 1962, Webb, S. pp.86-88).

Spencer related the tendency toward growing government intervention during the latter decades of the nineteenth century to competition between political parties for the votes of an extended electorate (In MacRae (ed), 1969, Spencer essay entitled The Coming Slavery). Intervention included health and educational reforms. He was most critical of the positive interventionism of Liberal governments. Spencer argued that they had betrayed the true liberal principles of restricting the state to the negative intervention of protecting individual rights from transgression in a free market economy (In MacRae (ed), 1969, Spencer essay entitled The New Toryism). The provision by the state of what should be left to individuals and their families to furnish represented for Spencer a waste of resources through inefficient meddling, the damaging imposition of standardization, and growing slavery to the state in the form of the work equivalent of the increased taxation required; a theme of all of his Man Versus the State essays (In MacRae (ed), 1969). Whilst Liberal governments were, from Spencer's viewpoint, abandoning true liberalism, the Conservatives were moving closer to supporting the free enterprise model.

Theoretical support for New Liberalism, a form of liberalism that viewed opportunities for the maximisation of individual freedom more in terms of its extension through state support rather than freedom from the state, came from T.H.Huxley who attacked Spencer's view that natural laws must form the basis for morality in a civilized society (Huxley, 1897, Prolegomena & Evolution and Ethics essay). He agreed with Spencer that 'survival of the fittest' was the evolutionary process operative in the organic world. It was also the dominant force during man's barbaric existence. However, there was, he argued, no justice in survival of the fittest. The advance of civilization required ethical codes guiding human action against the ravages of blind natural forces. Nature could know nothing of the moral ideals that man sets as the basis for progress. A measure of the progress of civilization would thus be man's capacity to provide a protective environment restraining the harsh operation of natural selection on man. Human progress would diverge from evolution in nature because there was a fundamental separation between intelligent human life and the rest of nature. Moreover, the failure of past intervention did not reflect the folly of intervention per se but instead the underdeveloped state of social science.

Similar insights were later developed by the New Liberal social theorist L.T. Hobhouse (Collini, 1979, pp.152-153) who argued that scientific sociology should be put to the service of intelligently controlling the working of natural evolution in the conscious pursuit of a progressive social ethic appropriate to man's civilised condition. This he referred to as 'orthogenic' evolution as opposed to allowing the blind forces of nature to prevail. Hobhouse's position placed less emphasis on heredity, thus enabling greater scope for intelligent social intervention whereby the state had a constructive role to play in removing obstacles in the way of individuals helping themselves.

Huxley likened man's ability to limit the operation of natural selection in society to that of a gardener controlling wild vegetation and creating a garden of his own design (Huxley, 1897, Prolegomena). To do so, the gardener needed to constantly guard his work against encroachments from nature. The implication of this analogy was that the state acted toward society as the gardener did toward his garden. A measure of social progress was the provision of a social environment in which a larger proportion of the weak could survive and the able enabled to rise above restricted life chances. This required welfare and educational intervention, the latter of which Huxley was strongly in favour of raising taxation on the individual to extend. To advocate natural selection as the basis for non-intervention would, from his viewpoint, represent a return to the law of the jungle, allowing, in the gardening analogy, wild vegetation to choke cultivated plants.

Spencer, with some justification, regarded such attacks on his scheme as based on distortions of his ideas. In reply to Huxley in his article Evolutionary Ethics (In Spencer, 1897), Spencer claimed that Huxley had misleadingly restricted attention to the ferocious aspect of competition which his laws of evolution showed would become progressively suspended as social evolution ran its course. As society evolved toward the industrial type, ferocious competition would be superseded by peaceful competition in which enlightened individuals, although competitive, would become mindful of each other's rights and freedoms. This would be no law of the jungle. Nevertheless, for J.S. Mill, the very appeal to the notion of nature as a guide to human behaviour was a dangerous one (In Mill, 1969, Mill's essay entitled Nature). Amongst its various connotations was the normality of behaviour based on instinct. Mill argued that civilization required rational standards of good behaviour to overcome man's anti-social instincts. In this case, civilization should intervene to challenge, not imitate, nature.

By the late nineteenth century, continental powers were advancing industrially and challenging Britain's ascendency. French and German industrialization were imitative, nationalistic and interventionist. During the long depression, industrial competition led to military competition for exploitation of colonies.

Spencer strongly opposed all war by industrial societies apart from in the clear case of defence against an aggressor (In Spencer, 1902, Spencer's article entitled Patriotism) and loathed the aggressiveness and distorting effect on the intellect of the sentiment 'our country, right or wrong'. He also argued that the benefits of the suppression of less advanced peoples were illusory. The militant external posture that was required enslaved the oppressors to their regulation of the oppressed abroad. It also enslaved the home population to increased taxation and regimentation of their lives and accompanied an upsurge of a barbaric mentality throughout society (In Spencer, 1902, Spencer's article entitled Imperialism and Slavery).

A new outlook on social evolution better reflected the times. Although the term 'social Darwinism' has been applied to a variety of theories of social evolution that place a high emphasis on heredity, including Spencer's own pre-Darwinian ideas, for Jones (1980), strictly speaking this term refers to theories which base evolution on conflict between societies. Those who adopted this position emphasised evolution through militancy. They opposed the disruptive effects of both organized labour and rational individualism on the well-being and potential for survival of the social organism under conditions of international aggression.

For Kidd (1894), the most evolved societies were those which utilized their human resources most efficiently. This required maximum equality of opportunity and inequality of reward. However, social superiority based on social efficiency required the subordination of rational individualism to the non-rational and self-sacrificing sentiment of patriotic duty. From this position, efficient and enlightened colonialism of those areas rich in resources and low in social efficiency, such as India, by advanced societies such as Britain (Kidd, 1894, Ch.10) could be justified as it would apparently benefit all.

A further reaction which allied evolution with militancy was the eugenics movement, originating in the works of Francis Galton. Eugenics theorists placed great emphasis on directly inherited and fixed genetic predisposition. From this viewpoint, the poor, whose reproduction rate was significantly higher than that of the middle classes, were regarded as genetically inferior to the latter. In this context, it was argued that the non-intervention which Spencer believed to represent a natural law of evolutionary benefit by allowing the poor and inadequate to wither away was not working. Indeed, they had proved to be the fittest in terms of reproduction. It was feared that a higher expansion rate amongst the poor would lead to the deterioration of the social stock. Ameliorative intervention in the plight of the poor, as advocated in New Liberalism, would lead to even greater overall deterioration. What, it was argued, was required to assist evolution, was some form of intervention based on precise knowledge of the laws of inheritance. In its most extreme form, the eugenicist Karl Pearson saw war as a form of genetic cleansing assisting the survival potential and enabling the triumph of advanced races.

By the end of the nineteenth century, changes in the international environment, the accompanying moral climate and dominant social theories had all assailed Spencer's industrial society and, in the hands of others, inverted his view of evolution. Spencer peered out dejected and helpless through the lens of his evolutionary theory in the realisation that no amount of reasoning in favour of enlightened individualism could stem the retrogression toward militancy.

9 | Herbert Spencer's Industrial Society

It is in his response to the French and Industrial Revolutions and the French Enlightenment that Spencer's social theory can be most clearly differentiated from the tradition of French positivists Saint Simon and Comte and against which Spencer's view of the viable social basis of the industrial society can be held up against that of Durkheim. Such differentiation shows that Durkheim's apparent refutation of Spencer was based on certain misrepresentations of Spencer's theory made through the lens of the French tradition. However, the author will show that a defence of Spencer's position, which was preoccupied with the opposite problem to that which haunted the French positivists, the problem of excessive social constraints on the individual, raises its own questions regarding individual freedom when considered from the point of view of explaining how social order was possible in the type of industrial society that he envisaged.

For Nisbet (1970b), a like reaction to the turmoil of the French Revolution and the English Industrial Revolution formed the social context of the foundation of sociology. These Revolutions raised concern with the problem of order in a new society and reawakened an interest in tradition. It is argued that sociology was founded on a significant reaction to the ideas of the Enlightenment and the social dislocations associated with modernization which followed it.

Nisbet's analysis would appear to offer quite an accurate appraisal of the origin and nature of French positivism. The latter inherited from the French Enlightenment its ontological idealism, the notion of progress and the appeal to reason. Early French positivists attempted to demonstrate that laws of intellectual and social progress pointed to the prospect of the rational reconstruction of society following Revolutionary upheaval. However, the ideas of the French Enlightenment were also analysed by Saint Simon and Comte as essentially responsible for the Revolution and the subsequent state of instability as a protracted condition of abnormality.

The French Catholic émigrés de Bonald and de Maistre strongly opposed the Enlightenment philosophes and viewed the Revolution and its aftermath of anarchy and attempted reconstruction as proof of man's essential wickedness and arrogance respectively. To curb the wickedness in human nature, they argued that a viable social order was not possible through rational human planning and only possible through a return to Catholic faith and the strong social constraints of the feudal social organism.

Saint Simon's positivism attempted to combine French Enlightenment and restorationist influences. He admired the social harmony which he associated with the feudal past but looked forward to a centrally regulated industrial society with a terrestrial orientated religion to replace Catholicism and promote a new level of social harmony. This emphasis on organicism and the enduring need for social constraints on the individual was a predominant element in the French positivist tradition in the context of the continuing social and political instabilities of the nineteenth century.

Comte's positivism retained the secular and scientific orientation of the Enlightenment. However, he held the critical ideas of the Enlightenment attack on theology to be responsible for the dissolution of the old social constraints and the collapse of social order. For Comte, as a matter of urgency the liberating effect of the Enlightenment had to be terminated. To this end, progress in his positivist scheme pointed to a systematic solution to the problem. Social analysis must be synthetic and constructive. The Enlightenment attack on church dogma was to be replaced by a secular orientated theology which converted the liberating emphasis of humanity associated with the Revolution to the ritualism and ceremonial constraints of the religion of humanity. Comte opposed the Enlightenment view of happiness maximization through the satisfaction of individual needs. Instead, the urgent need was to curtail the social morbidity of excessive egoism which collapse of old social structures and the loss of traditions had brought. The need for social constraints acquired a scientific justification and secular orientation in Comte's positivism which aimed to establish an intellectual basis for an orderly republic and a sociocracy.

Nisbet's analysis is somewhat less helpful in explaining the nature of Spencer's positivism. This is because he did not make sufficient distinction between the experiences of and reactions to the two Revolutions. Despite the social changes and the suffering associated with the Industrial Revolution, it did not represent the cataclysmic uprooting of old institutions as was the case with the French Revolution. This social context was therefore less conducive to a preoccupation with the need for social scientific rebuilding. And as a dissenter, Spencer was concerned more with the problem of excessive social constraints than that of the fear of disorder. He therefore held a relatively sympathetic orientation toward the Scottish Enlightenment.

Spencer fully endorsed the Enlightenment emphasis on individual rights and commercial modernization. He related happiness maximization to individual freedom and opposed the imposition of religious dogma and ritual as relics from the past. Spencer favoured the liberation of the individual from both traditional constraints or any other. As well as opposing religious, political and economic constraints, Spencer went as far as expressing antagonism toward the 'tyranny of conventions' (In Spencer, 1883a, Vol.1, essay entitled Manners and Fashion). However, he opposed certain aspects of the French Enlightenment which the French positivists had accepted. In particular, he opposed the view that ideas drive social change and that rational knowledge of the social whole could be the basis for interventionist reconstruction.

Like the French positivists, Spencer utilized the organic analogy. For Spencer, organicism pointed to the gradualism of natural growth. Ironically, organicism, along with his emphasis in *Social Statics* on divine 'beneficent necessity', made Spencer's early position superficially resemble that of the French Catholic writers who combined organicism with 'divine providence'. At this stage in his works, Spencer shared their contempt for the atheistic arrogance associated with the rational schemes of the French Enlightenment. However, in strong contrast to the Catholic writers and Comte's three stage model of progress in which the future resuscitated aspects of the past, progress and evolution for Spencer were framed within an essentially two stage model of linear advance away from the past. Spencer's scheme was conservative in the sense of its gradualist emphasis, but his theory was modernist from the point of view of the entrepreneurial middle classes and radically anti-aristocratic. In his reaction to the French Revolution, Spencer was more the Edmund Burke of the dissenting middle class.

Saint Simon and Comte combined a holistic view of society with their organicism. The notion that society was essentially just the product of an aggregate of individual actions was anathema to them. For Comte, the basic element of society had itself to be social. It was therefore the family (Martineau, 1855, Book 6, Ch.5). Viewing the health of society in holistic terms, the condition of all levels of society from element to entity was seen to be intimately related. Thus, it was not surprising that the social malaise of the Revolution was accompanied by an undermining of the family. In the positivist society, religious ritual and ceremony would be associated with the reconsolidation of society down to the basic social unit. In the reconstituted social order, Comte argued that the indissolubility of marriage would be re-established, and even came to demand perpetual widowhood (Comte, 1875, Vol.1, p.Xlii).

Spencer's methodological atomism placed him in the tradition of the Scottish Enlightenment writers, especially the political economists. He adopted a thoroughgoing atomism to all phenomena. For example, in explaining how this approach was applicable to the physical sciences, Spencer argued that the limits of physical structures are determined by the nature of the materials from which they are built. Similarly, he maintained that a viable social edifice is determined by the nature of the social element – the individuals making up society.

However, Spencer viewed society in its structure and growth as analogous to an organism. This analogy is difficult to reconcile with his atomism. Logically, as Dawe (1970) and Simon (1960) have commented, atomism lent itself to a view of society analogous to a mechanism fashioned from an aggregate of its elements. This view Spencer was usually keen to avoid because it implied a society of hard institutions which could be built and rebuilt according to rational design. The preferred alternative image of society as a complex organism whose workings were beyond the reach of detailed scientific knowledge allowed Spencer to combine non-interventionism with the gradualism of natural growth.

Was there a way out of this dilemma? Spencer occasionally used the mechanism analogy. When he did, it invariably related to the working of structured social institutions, especially the artefact of the state. Thus, regimented militant societies were more like mechanisms and de-regulated industrial societies of voluntary co-operation developed a plasticity analogous to an organism. The problem is that organicism implies holism and with holism is associated the emergent quality of the whole above being just the sum of its parts. In sociology, this position, as exemplified in the works of the French positivist Emile Durkheim, tends to lead to a reification of society as an overarching and constraining entity, the existence of which individuals serve. Yet Spencer applied organicism to the modern industrial society which he claimed existed for the benefit of the individual, not vice versa. Various writers (for example Gray, 1985; Wiltshire, 1978, Ch.9; Peel, 1971, Ch.7; Stark, 1961) have commented on the difficulties surrounding this apparent contradiction in Spencer's works.

French retrograde and Enlightenment influences were taken up in the sociology of Emile Durkheim. Durkheim's holistic approach to the study of society was in the tradition of his French predecessors Saint Simon and Comte. For Durkheim, society as a holistic entity was a higher level phenomena than an aggregate its individual elements, above whom it operated according to its own laws and over whom it exerted external constraint. This realm of external constraint was epitomised by the collective consciousness. It imposed the moral condition of society on the individual conscience. Vested in religious significance, the collective consciousness promoted social cohesion. The experience of a sacred external force which demanded the obedience of the individual therefore represented the moral constraints of the social entity that were necessary for the maintenance of social cohesion – a position that Durkheim fully developed in The Elementary Forms of the Religious Life (1976). For Durkheim, effective moral integration represented a healthy social condition, especially as it had to counter the disruptive effect on society of the advancing division of labour that accompanied modernization.

Durkheim was highly critical of Spencer's methodological atomism. For Spencer, he claimed, social justice in the ultimate industrial society required only that individuals honour contracts freely entered into and not transgress the like rights of other individuals. Durkheim considered that if this were realized, Spencer's industrial society would comprise a

'vast system of particular contracts which link individuals.......
They would depend upon the group only in proportion to their dependence upon one another, and they would depend upon one another only in proportion to conventions privately entered into and freely concluded. Social solidarity would then be nothing else than the spontaneous accord of individual interests, an accord of which contracts are the natural expression. The typical social relation would be the economic, stripped of all regulation and resulting from the entirely free initiative of the parties' (Durkheim, 1964a, p.203).

With Hobbesian insight, Durkheim then pressed home the point.

'where interest is the only ruling force each individual finds himself in a state of war with every other since nothing comes to mollify the egos, and any truce in this eternal antagonism would not be of long duration. There is nothing less constant than interest. Today, it unites me to you; tomorrow it will make me your enemy' (Durkheim, 1964a, pp.203-204).

Given the advance of the division of labour, the intensity of competition and the rising living standards which accompany industrialization, this degree of release of the individual from social constraints would be disastrous for the social organism and consequently individuals. It would constitute a loss of anchorage for individual appetites and expectations in a more meritocratic and materialistic society, providing an environment prone to the social malaise of high levels of individual dissatisfaction. A 'society' based on economic individualism would constitute the preoccupation of individuals in the world of the profane. The necessary external constraints of the sacred on individual behaviour would be absent. Such unbounded individual freedom would therefore be far from maximizing individual happiness. For Durkheim, it would represent the perpetuation of a pathological condition to which societies having made rapid change to the early stage of modernisation are prone, taking the form of anomie (a malintegrated society of unstable and uncertain social norms) and egoism (a dangerous level of self-absorption through lack of the integration of individuals into social groups).

This viewpoint and criticism indicated a fundamental distinction between Spencer and the French positivists concerning a viable basis for social cohesion in the modern industrial society. We need to return to Spencer's work to appreciate that Durkheim offered an inadequate representation of his position. As a social holist and emphasising the emergent nature of social phenomena, Durkheim viewed the social and moral realm as something existing external to the individual. The state of the collective consciousness would be internalized by the individual. Importantly, for Durkheim, social change did not amount to moral evolution in an inbuilt biological sense.

Like Hobbes, Spencer was an atomist. The form that social cohesion must take was determined by the moral condition of individuals. Spencer acknowledged that a state of callous egoism required the imposition of social constraints: 'what a cage is to the wild beast, law is to the selfish man' (Spencer, 1970, p.14). But he viewed the moral condition as gradually modifiable through the inheritance of acquired characteristics influenced over long periods of time by environment. The nature of social cohesion would thus gradually change with the moral modification of the individual units upon which society is based. Enlightenment was therefore at root a moral condition rather than an intellectual one. Laws of evolution and progress indicated social environmental changes conducive to the advance of enlightened individualism. This moral condition would ultimately provide a sound basis upon which a society of contractual relationships between individuals could rest. To work toward this condition, the role of the state should gradually be restricted to that of negative intervention – the guaranteeing of justice in the form of the protection of the rights of the individual from transgression by others, as long as the moral condition required this.

This contraction of state intervention would appear to be harsh in matters of welfare given the misfortunes of life that can affect people. But Spencer increasingly emphasised that enlightened individualism was the highest form of egoism. For Spencer, the tendency for individuals to find satisfaction in the assistance of deserving others was a mark of growing moral sensitivity. Referred to as beneficence, it comprised the assistance of individuals beyond the strict requirements of justice. Beneficent action of individuals toward others could take a positive form (Spencer,

1978, Vol.2, Pt.5) such as the provision of pecuniary assistance to the deserving needy, or in a negative form (Spencer, 1978, Vol.2, Pt.6) it could include such decisions as to refrain from belittling others through displays of individual ability or avoiding attribution of blame to others by taking circumstances into account. By assimilating altruism into egoism at the advanced moral stage, the charge of resultant social disunity which would derive from primitive callous egoism under conditions of deregulation could be avoided. Durkheim failed to recognize Spencer's theory of individual moral evolution and the morality of beneficence.

By relating the origin and essence of religion to the social whole, Durkheim (1976) had emphasised the enduring need for ritual and symbolism to orientate the individual to society. His rationalist study of religion secularized these aspects of the French Catholic heritage. By demonstrating religion to be the worship of society transfigured as opposed to Comte's more abstract notion of the religion of humanity (Durkheim, 1973, Ch.5), Durkheim's theory was conducive to the nationalism of the French Third Republic.

Spencer, by contrast, traced the origin of religion to the mind of the individual (Spencer, 1885a, Vol.1, Pt.1). He argued that religion originated in the primitive notion of spirit doubles which was suggested to individuals by the experience of dreams. Once man deduced from these experiences a belief in a spirit world, the form that religion took would vary with man's social and moral condition. The external constraints of ceremony and ritual were a necessary complement to the moral condition of callous egoism under militancy. However, ceremony and ritual did not serve an enduring need. Indeed, evolution toward enlightened individualism required their demise. Progressive individualism in the economic sphere would be naturally complemented by religious dissent which allowed room for individual independent thought in religious matters. This analysis equated modernism with the individualism of the dissenting middle class and opposed the ceremony and symbolism of Catholicism which remained as a secularized survival in French positivism. Ultimately, for Spencer, religion would persist not because it related to an ever needed social function of the collective consciousness but as a result of an awareness of the unconditioned unknown in the consciousness of individuals which advances in knowledge will never overcome.

Spencer looked forward to a society of acquisitive individualism comprising private property ownership and in which individual enterprise provided material reward. In such a society, large institutions would be absent. There would be no room for the regulative apparatus of a central bank and financial institutions would not have privileged protection from bankruptcy (In Spencer, 1883b, Vol.2, essay entitled State Tamperings with Money and Banks). The economy would be left to self-regulate, the state would have all but withered away and levels of taxation would be miniscule. The provision of education would be a matter of parental responsibility and the use of small independent organisations. Health care would be delivered through the private sector and the provision of welfare would be left to the judgement of beneficent individuals on a case by case basis.

In addressing what Spencer saw as the problem of social constraints, he portrayed his future industrial society as evolving to a new level of cohesion; a society of enlightened individuals ultimately free from all external constraints; one of the ownership of the self and the evolution of moral responsibility of individuals for the consequences of their own actions. But defence of Spencer against those more concerned with the problem of order raises the question – what would really be the scope of individual 'freedom' in Spencer's industrial society? Spencer maintained that moral evolution to enlightened individualism would make man instinctively obedient to the law of equal freedom (Spencer, 1978, Vol.1, Pt.1, Ch.7). Arguably, and in line with a similar point raised by Wiltshire (1978) in the context of efficiency, the degree of internal moral constraint necessary for social cohesion in Spencer's industrial society would need to be so great as to render the individual's actions less free than in a society where the individual is controlled by external social constraints which he or she may resist.

Bibliography

Abrams, P. (1968) *The Origins of British Sociology: 1834–1914.* London: University of Chicago Press.

Acton, H.B. (1951) 'Comte's Positivism and the Science of Society.' *Philosophy,* 26 (No.99), pp.291-310.

Anderson, P. (1984) *Lineages of the Absolutist State.* London: Verso.

Andreski, S. (1972) *Herbert Spencer.* London: Nelson.

Barrington Moore Jr (1967) *The Social Origins of Dictatorship and Democracy.* Harmondsworth: Penguin.

Bogardus, E.S. (1940) *The Development of Social Thought.* New York: McKay.

Bottomore, T. & Nisbet, R.A. (ed) (1978) *A History of Sociological Analysis.* London: Heinemann.

Bowle, J. (1954) *Politics and Opinion in the Nineteenth Century.* London: Jonathan Cape.

Brebner, J.B. (1948) 'Laissez Faire and State Intervention in Nineteenth-Century Britain.' *Journal of Economic History,* 8 (1), pp.59-73.

Briggs, A. (1956) 'Middle-Class Consciousness in English Politics, 1780-1846'. *Past and Present,* 9 (1), pp.65-74.

Brinton, C. (1933) *English Political Thought in the Nineteenth Century.* London: Ernest Benn.

Brinton, C. (1937) 'Spencer's Horrid Vision.' *Foreign Affairs*, 15.

Brown, P.A. (1918) *The French Revolution in English History.* London: Crosby Lockwood.

Brumfitt, J.H. (1972) *The French Enlightenment.* London: Macmillan.

Burrow, J.W. (1968) *Evolution and Society.* Cambridge: Cambridge University Press.

Bury, J.B. (1920) *The Idea of Progress: An Inquiry into its Origin and Growth.* London: Macmillan.

Butler, E.M. (1926) *The Saint-Simonian Religion in Germany.* Cambridge: Cambridge University Press.

Carneiro, R.L. (1967) *Herbert Spencer: The Evolution of Society.* Chicago & London: University of Chicago Press.

Charlton, D.G. (1959) *Positivist Thought in France During the Second Empire, 1852–1870.* Oxford: Clarendon Press.

Charlton, D.G. (1963) *Secular Religions in France, 1815-1870.* London: Oxford University Press.

Chitnis, A.C. (1976) *The Scottish Enlightenment.* London: Croom Helm.

Cobban, A. (1974) *The Social Interpretation of the French Revolution.* London: Cambridge University Press.

Collini, S. (1979) *Liberalism and Sociology.* Cambridge: Cambridge University Press.

Comte, A. (1874) *The Catechism of Positive Religion.* London: Trubner.

Comte, A (1875) *The System of Positive Polity* (4 Volumes). New York: Burt Franklin.

Coser, L.A. (1977) *Masters of Sociological Thought.* New York: Harcourt Brace Jovanovich.

Cowherd, R.G. (1959) *The Politics of English Dissent.* New York: New York University Press.

Dawe, A. (1970) 'The Two Sociologies.' *British Journal of Sociology*, 21 (2), pp.207-218.

Dennis, B. & Skilton, D. (1978) *Reform and Intellectual Debate in Victorian England.* London: Croom Helm.

Desmond, A. & Moore, J. (1991) *Darwin.* London: Michael Joseph.

Dickinson, G.L. (1927) *Revolution and Restoration in Modern France.* London: George Allen & Unwin.

Duncan, D. (1908) *The Life and Letters of Herbert Spencer.* London: Methuen.

Depeux, G. (1967) *French Society 1789-1979.* London: Methuen.

Durkheim, E. (1959) *Socialism and Saint Simon.* London: Routledge & Kegan Paul.

Durkheim, E. (1964a) *The Division of Labour in Society.* New York: Free Press.

Durkheim, E. (1964b) *The Rules of Sociological Method.* New York and London: Free Press.

Durkheim, E (1970) *Suicide.* London: Routledge.

Durkheim, E. (1973) *Moral Education.* London: The Free Press.

Durkheim, E. (1976) *The Elementary Forms of the Religious Life.* London: George Allen & Unwin.

Eisen, S. (1968) 'Frederic Harrison and Herbert Spencer: Embattled Unbelievers.' *Victorian Studies*, 12 (1), pp.33-56.

Engels, F. (1974) *The Condition of the Working Class in England.* St.Albans: Panther.

Ferri, E. (1905) *Socialism and Positive Science.* London: Independent Labour Party.

Feyerabend, P, (1975) *Against method: Outline of an Anarchistic Theory of Knowledge.* London: New Left Books.

Fielden, K. (1968) 'Samuel Smiles and Self-Help.' *Victorian Studies*, 12 (2), pp.155-176.

Fletcher, R. (1974) *The Crisis of Industrial Civilisation: The Early Essays of Auguste Comte.* London: Heinemann.

George, H. (1893) *A perplexed Philosopher.* London: Kegan Paul, Trench and Traubner.

Giddens, A. (1974) *Positivism and Sociology.* London: Heinemann.

Giddens, A. (1977) *New Rules of Sociological Method.* London: Hutchinson.

Ginsberg, M. (1973) *The Idea of Progress: A Revaluation.* Westport, Connecticut: Greenwood Press.

Gould, J.F. (1920) *Auguste Comte.* London: Watts.

Gouldner, A.W. (1977) *The Coming Crisis of Western Sociology.* London: Heinemann.

Gray, A. (1946) *The Socialist Tradition: Moses to Lenin.* London: Longmare, Green & C.

Gray, T.S. (1985) 'Herbert Spencer: Individualist or Organicist.' *Political Studies*, 33 (2), pp.236-253.

Green, F.C. (1965) *A Comparative View of French and British Civilisation, 1850-1870.* London: Dent.

Gregg, P. (1984) *A Social and Economic History of Britain, 1760-1980.* London: Harrap.

Gruner, S.M. (1973) *Economic Materialism and Social Moralism.* The Hague: Mouton.

Haight, G.S. (1969) *George Eliot. A Biography.* London: Oxford University Press.

Haines, V.A. (1988) 'Is Spencer's Theory an Evolutionary Theory?' *American Journal of Sociology*, 93 (5), pp.1200-1223.

Halfpenny, P. (1982) *Positivism and Sociology.* London: George Allen & Unwin.

Hampson, N.H. (1963) *A Social History of the French Revolution.* London: Routledge and Kegan Paul.

Haralambos, M., & Holborn, M. (2000) *Sociology: Themes and Perspectives.* London: Collins.

Hayek, F.A. (1952) *The Counter Revolution of Science.* Illinois: Free Press.

Hewett, C. (2008) *Henri de Saint-Simon.* Available at: www.thegreatdebate.org.uk/saint-simon.html (Accessed 19/1/2015).

Hobsbawm, E.J. (1974) *Industry and Empire.* Harmondsworth: Penguin.

Huxley, T.H. (1893) *Methods and Results.* London: Macmillan.

Huxley, T.H. (1897) *Evolution and Ethics and Other Essays.* New York: Appleton.

Iggers, G.G. (1958) *The Cult of Authority.* The Hague: Martinus Nijhoff.

Ionescu, G. (1976) *The Political Thought of Saint Simon.* London: Oxford University Press.

James, W. (1911) *Memories and Studies.* London: Longmans, Green and Co.

Jones, G. (1980) *Social Darwinism and English Thought.* Brighton: Harvester Press.

Jones, R.A. (1974) 'Durkheim's Response to Spencer: An Essay Toward Historicism in the Historiography of Sociology.' *The Sociological Quarterly*, 15 (3), pp.341-359.

Kandiner, A. & Preble, E. (1962) *They Studied Man.* London: Secker & Warburg.

Kidd, B. (1894) *Social Evolution.* London: Macmillan.

Kilminster, R. (2014) 'The Debate about Utopias from a Sociological Perspective.' *Human Figurations* 3 (2). Available at http://quod.lib. umich.edu/h/humfig/11217607.0003.2*?rgn=full+text (Accessed 14/2/2015).

Kitson Clark, G. (1967) *An Expanding Society.* Cambridge: Cambridge University Press.

Kuhn, T (1962) *The Structure of Scientific Revolutions.* Chicago: University of Chicago Press.

Kumar, K (1987) *Prophecy and progress.* Harmondsworth: Penguin.

Kumar, K. (1991) *Utopianism.* Buckingham: Open University Press.

Lincoln, A. (1971) *Some Political and Social Ideas of English Dissent, 1763-1800.* New York: Octagon Books.

Lively, J. (1965) *The Works of Joseph de Maistre.* London: George Allen & Unwin.

Lukes, S. (1968) 'Methodological Individualism Reconsidered.' *British Journal of Sociology*, 19 (2), pp.119-129.

MacLeod, R.M. (1970) 'The X-Club. A Social Network of Science in Late-Victorian England.' *Notes and Records of the Royal Society of London*, 24 (2), pp.305-322.

MacRae, D.G. (ed.) (1969) *Spencer, the Man Versus the State.* Harmondsworth: Penguin.

Spencer's essays from this publication referred to in this text, with original publication dates:

The New Toryism (1884)

The Coming Slavery (1884)

The Sins of Legislators (1884)

The Great Political Superstition (1884)

From Freedom to Bondage (1891)

McCord, N. (1958) *The Anti-Corn Law League.* London: George Allen & Unwin.

McLeod, H. (1996) *Religion and Society in England, 1850-1914.* Basingstoke: MacMillan

McPhee, P. (1992) *A Social History of France, 1780-1880.* London: Routledge.

Manuel, F. (1963) *The New World of Henri Saint Simon.* Indiana: University of Notre Dame Press.

Manuel, F. (1965) *The Prophets of Paris.* New York: Harper & Row.

Markham, F. (1952) *Saint Simon: Selected Writings.* Oxford: Blackwell.

Martineau, H. (1855) *The Positive Philosophy of Auguste Comte.* New York: Calvin Blanchard.

Maus, H. (1962) *A Short History of Sociology.* London: Routledge & Kegan Paul.

Merton, R.K. (1970) *Science, Technology and Society in Seventeenth Century England.* New York: Howard Fertig.

Mill, J.S. (1865) *Auguste Comte and Positivism.* London: Trubner.

Mill, J.S. (1969) *Essays on Ethics, Religion and Society.* London: Routledge & Kegan Paul.

Moody, J.N. (1953) *Church and Society.* New York: Arts Inc.

Monet, D. (1969) *French Thought in the Eighteenth Century.* Connecticut: Archon Books.

Nisbet, R.A. (1970a) *Social Change and History.* New York: Oxford University Press.

Nisbet, R.A. (1970b) *The Sociological Tradition.* London: Heinemann.

Normano, J.F. (1932) 'Saint-Simon and America.' *Social Forces*, 11 (1), p.8.

Offer, J.W. (1980) 'Interpreting Spencer.' *Sociology*, 14 (1), pp.131-140.

Offer, J.W. (1983) 'Spencer's Sociology of Welfare.' *The Sociological Review*, 31 (4), pp.719-752.

Open University (1974) *Scientific Progress and Religious Dissent.* Milton Keynes: Open University Press.

Peel, J.D.Y. (1971) *Herbert Spencer, the Evolution of a Sociologist.* London: Heinemann.

Perkin, H. (1972) *The Origins of Modern British Society, 1780-1880.* London: Routledge.

Perkin, H. (1989) *The Rise of Professional Society.* London: Routledge.

Perrin, R.G. (1976) 'Herbert Spencer's Four Theories of Social Evolution.' *American Journal of Sociology*, 81 (6), pp.1339-1359.

Polanyi, K. (1947) 'On Belief in Economic Determinism.' *The Sociological Review*, 39 (1), pp. 96-102.

Pollard, S. (1971) *The Idea of Progress.* Harmondsworth: Penguin.

Popper, K.R. (1972) *Conjectures and Refutations.* London: Routledge & Kegan Paul.

Popper, K.R. (1974) *The Poverty of Historicism.* London: Routledge & Kegan Paul.

Price, R. (1987) *A Social History of Nineteenth-Century France.* London: Hutchionson.

Pullinger, J.T. (2014) *Sociological Thinking A New Introduction.* Cambridge: Cambridge Academic.

Rayner, R.M. (1962) *Nineteenth Century England.* London: Longmans.

Read, D. (1964) *The English Provinces.* London and Southampton: Camelot Press.

Roark, E. (2004) 'Herbert Spencer's Evolutionary Individualism.' *Quarterly Journal of Ideology,* 27 (3 & 4), pp.1-31.

Robertson, J.M. (1927) *Modern Humanists Reconsidered.* London: Watts.

Robinson, E. (1953) 'The Derby Philosophical Society.' *Annals of Science,* 9 (3), pp.359-367.

Rumney, J. (1966) *Herbert Spencer's Sociology.* New York: Atherton Press.

Sahlins, M.D. & Service, E.R. (1973) *Evolution and Culture.* University of Michigan Press.

Salvemini, G. (1963) *The French Revolution, 1788-1792.* London: Jonathan Cape.

Schapiro, J.S. (1948) *Liberalism and the Challenge of Fascism.* New York: McGraw-Hill.

Schofield, R.E. (1963) *The Lunar Society of Birmingham.* London: Oxford University Press.

Shaw, G.B. (1900) *Fabianism and Empire.* London: Grant Richards.

Simon, W.M. (1956) 'History for Utopia: Saint-Simon and the Idea of Progress.' *Journal of the History of Ideas,* 17 (3), pp.311-331.

Simon, W.M. (1960) 'Herbert Spencer and the "Social Organism".' *Journal of the History of Ideas,* 21 (2), pp.294-299.

Sokoloff, B. (1975) *The 'Mad' Philosopher Auguste Comte.* Connecticut: Greenwood Press.

Somervell, D.C. (1929) *English Thought in the Nineteenth Century.* London: Methuen.

Sorokin, P.A. (1963) *Modern Historical and Social Philosophies.* New York: Dover Publications.

Spencer, H. (1842) Essays on 'The Proper Sphere of Government,' *The Nonconformist,* 1842.

Spencer, H. (1861) *Education*. London: G. Manwaring.

Spencer's essays from this publication referred to in this text, with original publication dates:

   Intellectual Education (May, 1854)

   Moral Education (April 1858)

   Physical Education (April 1859)

   What Knowledge is of Most Worth? (July, 1859)

Spencer, H. (1874-1934) *Descriptive Sociology*. London: Williams & Norgate.

Spencer, H. (1877) 'Mr. Tylor's Review of The Principles of Sociology.' *Mind*, 2, pp.415-418.

Spencer, H. (1878) *Essays: Scientific, Political and Speculative, Vol.3.* London: Williams & Norgate.

Spencer's essays from this publication referred to in this text, with original publication dates:

   The Classification of the Sciences (April, 1864)

   Reasons for Dissenting from the Philosophy of M. Comte (1864)

   Political Fetichism (June 1865)

   The Origin of Animal Worship (May 1870)

   Specialized Administration (December 1871)

   Mr. Martineau on Evolution (June 1872)

Spencer, H. (1880) *The Study of Sociology*. London: Williams & Norgate.

Spencer, H. (1883a) *Essays: Scientific, Political and Speculative, Vol.1.* London: Williams & Norgate.

Spencer's essays from this publication referred to in this text, with original publication dates:

   The Development Hypothesis (March 1852)

   Manners and Fashion (April 1854)

The Genesis of Science (July 1854)

Progress: its Law and Cause (April 1857)

The Social Organism (January 1860)

Spencer, H. (1883b) *Essays: Scientific, Political and Speculative, Vol.2.* London: Williams & Norgate.

Spencer's essays from this publication referred to in this text, with original publication dates:

Over-Legislation (July 1853)

Railway Morals and Railway Policy (October 1854)

State Tamperings with Money and Banks (January 1858)

The Morals of Trade (April 1859)

Parliamentary Reform: the Dangers and the Safeguards (April 1860)

Prison Ethics (July 1860)

Spencer, H. (1883c) *The Principles of Sociology, Vol.2, Pt.4, Spencer on Ceremonial Institutions.* London: Williams & Norgate.

Spencer, H. (1884) 'Retrogressive Religion.' *Popular Science Monthly,* 25, pp.451-474.

Spencer, H. (1885a) *The Principles of Sociology, Vol.1, Pts.1-3, Spencer on Sociology.* London: Williams & Norgate.

Spencer, H. (1885b) *The Principles of Sociology, Vol.2, Pt.5, Political Institutions.* London: Williams & Norgate.

Spencer, H. (1885c) *The Principles of Sociology, Vol.3, Pt.6, Spencer on Ecclesiastical Institutions.* London: Williams & Norgate.

Spencer, H. (1897) *Various Fragments,* London: Williams & Norgate.

Spencer's articles from this publication referred to in this text:

An Element in Method

M. de Laveleye's Error

Professor Tait on the Formula of Evolution

Views Concerning Copyright

Spencer, H. (1901) *The Principles of Sociology, Vol.1, includes:*

Lord Salisbury on Evolution (November 1895)

Spencer, H. (1902) *Facts and Comments*. London: Williams & Norgate.

Spencer's articles from this publication referred to in this text:

Barbaric Art

Imperialism and Slavery

Patriotism

Re-Barbarization

Spontaneous Reform

Vaccination

Spencer, H. (1904) *An Autobiography, Volumes 1 & 2*. London: Williams & Norgate.

Spencer, H. (1910) *Social Statics, Abridged and Revised*. London: Watts.

Spencer, H. (1946) *First Principles*. London: Watts.

Spencer, H. (1968) *Reasons for Dissenting from the Philosophy of M. Comte and Other Essays*. Berkeley: Glendessary Press.

Spencer, H. (1970) *Social Statics*. Farnborough: Gregg International.

Spencer, H. (1975) *The Principles of Sociology, Vol.3, Pts.6-8, Ecclesiastical Institutions, Professional Institutions and Industrial Institutions*. Westport Connecticut: Greenwood Press.

Spencer, H. (1978) *The Principles of Ethics, Vol.1, Pts.1-3, Vol.2, Pts.4-6.* Indianapolis: Liberty Classics.

Stark, W. (1961) 'Herbert Spencer's Three Sociologies.' *American Sociological Review*, 26 (4), pp.515-521.

Szacki, J. (1980) 'Reflections on the History of Sociology.' *The Polish Sociological Bulletin*, 52 (4), pp.5-15.

Taylor, K. (1975) *Henri Saint-Simon*. London: Croom Helm.

Thompson, E.P. (1974) *The Making of the English Working Class*. Harmondsworth: Penguin.

Thompson, K. (1976) *Auguste Comte: The Foundation of Sociology.* London: Nelson.

Thomson, J.A. (1906) *English Men of Science: Herbert Spencer.* London: J.M.Dent.

Tocqueville, A. de (1966) *The Ancien Regime and the French Revolution.* Manchester: Fontana.

Tylor, E.B. (1877) 'Mr. Spencer's Principles of Sociology.' *Mind*, 2, pp.141-155.

Ward, L.F. (1909) 'The Career of Herbert Spencer.' *The Popular Science Monthly*, 74, pp.5-18.

Watson, G. (1973) *The English Ideology.* London: Allen Lane.

Webb, B. (1950) *My Apprenticeship.* London: Longmans.

Webb, S. et al (1962) *Fabian Essays.* London: George Allen & Unwin.

Weber, M. (1978) *The Protestant Ethic and the Spirit of Capitalism.* London: George Allen & Unwin.

Wiener, J.W. (1981) *English Culture and the Decline of the Industrial Spirit.* Cambridge: Cambridge University Press.

Williams, E.N. (1970) *The Ancien Regime in Europe.* Harmondsworth: Penguin Books.

Wiltshire, D. (1978) *The Social and Political Thought of Herbert Spencer.* Oxford: Oxford University Press.

Wolf, J.B. (1963) *France: 1814-1919.* New York, Evanston and London: Harper & Row.

Wright, G. (1981) *France in Modern Times.* New York: W.W.Norton.

Young, R.M. (1985) *Darwin's Metaphor: Nature's Place in Victorian Culture.* Cambridge: Cambridge University Press.

Zeitlin, I.M. (1968) *Ideology and the Development of Sociological Theory.* New Jersey: Prentice-Hall.

Index